Nice 'n Easy
■ French ■
Grammar

avoir - to have (perfect)

être - to be

faire - to do

pouvoir - to have (future)

Nice 'n Easy ■ French ■ Grammar

C. BESWICK

PASSPORT BOOKS
a division of *NTC Publishing Group*
Lincolnwood, Illinois USA

Also available

Nice 'n Easy German Grammar
Nice 'n Easy Spanish Grammar

1993 Printing

This edition first published in 1985 by Passport Books,
a division of NTC Publishing Group, 4255 West Touhy
Avenue, Lincolnwood (Chicago), Illinois 60646-1975 U.S.A.
Originally published by Pan Books Ltd, © C. Beswick
1983. All rights reserved. No part of this book may
be reproduced, stored in a retrieval system, or transmitted
in any form, or by any means, electronic, mechanical, photocopying,
or otherwise, without the prior written permission
of NTC Publishing Group.
Manufactured in the United States of America.

3 4 5 6 7 8 9 ML 9 8 7 6 5

Contents

Using this book

The word 'grammar' is generally guaranteed to discourage people from learning a foreign language, so why a basic grammar book for travelers? Is it possible to make yourself understood without bothering about grammar rules?

The answer to that is 'Yes, to a certain extent.' A good phrasebook can help you to get by, but unless you know some of the rules about how the language is put together, you are tied down to the particular word or phrase in your book. *Understanding the grammar rules enables you to 'create' new language and say things which are not in your phrasebook.*

This book is designed to help you sort out the most important rules which you will need to speak and understand French in everyday situations. It does not deal with grammar just for the sake of it, but with specific communication tasks in mind – seeking a service or information, saying what you require, and asking permission are a few examples.

You can cope very well with the grammar of your own language without ever having to worry what a noun or an adjective does. Why bother then with terms like noun, adjective and pronoun in a foreign language? The answer is that such terms do save time by avoiding the need to keep on explaining the function or job of a particular item of grammar. This is important for the purpose of getting your message through. To help you understand these shorthand terms, there is a *Grammar glossary* beginning on p.8, which is short enough to read in one sitting before starting any of the other sections in the book.

The *Topic index* on p.135 gives you information on which sections of the book are useful for coping with a particular situation, e.g. asking the way, choosing between different items when shopping, describing something you've lost, and explaining that you don't feel well.

The *Grammatical index* on p.131 gives you information about where to look for the explanation of a particular grammar point, e.g. nouns, verbs, adjectives and pronouns, including the original definition of such terms in the *Grammar glossary*.

Once you have found the section which interests you, you will be given
● a clear explanation
● examples from everyday speech and written language

If you wish to practice certain points of grammar, you can work from the *Try it yourself* (TIY) section on p.78. Practice from this section will help you as a business or vacation traveler, rather than help you to pass traditional examinations in French. You can check your answers against those in the *Answers* section starting on p.112.

There is neither space nor time in this book to give you any guide to pronunciation. A good phrasebook will give you some help, as will obtaining some of the commercially produced cassettes which are on the market, taking a radio or television language course or finding the time to join a local adult-education class.

Glossary of grammar terms

This section of the book has deliberately been made short enough for you to read it through in one session before you start dipping into the main section of the book. The aim is to familiarize you with some of the grammar terms which will be used. One explanation in this glossary will save having to repeat the explanation several times in different parts of the book.

The explanations given in this section are not always precise, academic definitions. They are meant to help you understand that grammar is really all about communication in a foreign language, in other words getting your message across. For this reason the terms are not listed in alphabetical order, but grouped together in ways which should simplify the explanations rather than make you an expert on grammatical definitions!

All the examples given in the glossary are from English.

NOUN Generally a word which makes sense with 'a' or 'the' in front of it. It could be the label we attach to a thing, a place or an idea, e.g. pen, garden, love.

PROPER NOUN Usually the name of a person or place, spelled with a capital letter at the beginning of the word, e.g. Paul, America.

PRONOUN A word which stands for or replaces a noun or proper noun and possibly certain words connected with such a noun. A pronoun is nearly always shorter than the noun it replaces and therefore saves time when speaking, e.g.

Have you seen *my old jacket?*
Yes, *it*'s in the closet.

VERB A word used to denote an action, state or event, e.g.

he *was shaving*
I *am* happy here
the film *started* three hours ago

TENSE Verbs have different tenses to show the *time* of the action, state or event, e.g.

he's *playing* tennis right now   (present tense NOW)
he *played* tennis last week   (past tense IN THE PAST)
he *will play* again next Tuesday   (future tense IN THE FUTURE)

PERSONS Verbs in a foreign language are normally printed in a pattern with six persons:

Singular		*Plural*	
I	1st	we	1st
you	2nd	you	2nd
he/she/it	3rd	they	3rd

The persons in the left-hand column are called *singular* because they refer to only one person. The persons in the right-hand column are called *plural* because they refer to more than one person. So, 1st person singular = 'I', 1st person plural = 'we', 3rd person singular = 'he', 'she', 'it', etc.

Although you are not aware of it in your own language, the person controls the spelling of the verb, e.g.

1st person singular   I shout
3rd person singular   he shout<u>s</u>

SUBJECT A noun or pronoun is said to be the subject of the sentence when it is the originator or performer of the action, state or happening:

he was shaving   (he was the one doing the shaving)
I am happy   (I am the one who is happy)
the *film* started   (it was the film that started)

OBJECT A noun or pronoun is said to be the object of the sentence when it is on the receiving end of the action:

the barber shaved *him*   (he was the one being shaved)
the projectionist started the *film*   (it was the film which was started)

REGULAR VERB A regular verb fits in with a pattern which many other verbs follow, e.g. in English many verbs add '-ed' to form their past tense:

to hand   he hand*ed* me the book
to play   he play*ed* well that time
to look   he look*ed* all over for her

IRREGULAR VERB An irregular verb does not fit into a predictable pattern, but rather sets its own individual pattern:

to see: would be 'he seed' if regular in the past tense, but in fact is *he saw*

to think: would be 'he thinked' if regular in the past tense, but in fact is *he thought*

to read: would be 'he readed' if regular in the past tense, but in fact is *he read*

FINITE VERB A finite verb is controlled by a subject, in so far as the verb will change if the subject changes. The verb in the sentence 'I play the violin' will change if the subject is changed from 'I' to 'he' ('he play*s* the violin').

Often you are not aware of changes like this in your own language but you should be much more conscious of them in a foreign language. In most complete sentences there has to be a finite verb somewhere, and the spelling and pronunciation of that verb will be controlled by the subject.

INFINITIVE An infinitive is not controlled by a subject. In English an infinitive normally has 'to' in front of it, e.g. 'to work', 'to play', 'to be', etc. The infinitive does not change when the subject changes, e.g.

I am learning *to play* the guitar
you are learning *to play* the guitar
he is learning *to play* the guitar

The infinitive remains the same even if you change the subject an infinite number of times. In a foreign language the infinitive is the spelling of the verb which you will find in a dictionary or word list. You cannot use the infinitive on its own in a sentence. It has to be used with some other verb which is finite and therefore governed by a subject.

AUXILIARY VERB Since auxiliary means 'helping' or 'assistant' (as in Auxiliary Fire Department) an 'auxiliary verb' helps to form a tense by combining with another verb or part of a verb:

I *have* seen that film
she *was* waiting
I *will* see you later

PARTICIPLE This is a part of a verb which generally has to be used with another verb rather than being able to stand on its own. You can see in the following sentence that the two participles (one a *past* participle referring to what *has* happened, and one a *present* participle, referring to what is happening *now*) sound odd if left on their own.

he stolen that man's wallet and now he running away

The sentence becomes complete only when the auxiliary verbs 'has' and 'is' are included:

he *has* stolen that man's wallet and now he *is* running away

VERB ENDINGS AND STEM In English, verbs have fewer extra letters added on at the end than in many foreign languages, although the 3rd person singular, for example, requires an '-s' to be added to verbs in the present tense:

I work   he work*s*
I sing   he sing*s*

In French there will be more endings to remember. In most tenses there is a part of the verb which will remain the same. This base part of the verb is called the 'stem'. The letters which are added to this base part and which will change according to the subject (I, you, he, we etc) are called the 'endings'.

DEFINITE, INDEFINITE AND PARTITIVE ARTICLES The article is the short word appearing before a noun which can be of three types:
1 the definite article: *the* book
(definite because it refers to a specific or definite book)
2 the indefinite article: either *a* book or *some* books
(indefinite because it does not refer to a particular or definite book or books)
3 the partitive article: either *some* books (partitive because it refers to a part, portion or quantity of – for example, cheese, rather than a whole cheese).

GENDER Often this is clearly connected with the sex of a person or animal, i.e. male or female. The gender of English nouns is sometimes clear, e.g. wait*er*, wait*ress*, but on the whole we are not conscious of gender as a *pervasive* concept in language. In French *all* nouns, whether they are the names of human beings or not, are given a 'gender'. You will see the gender indicated by *m.* (masculine) or *fem.* (feminine) in dictionaries. The article in front of the noun also frequently indicates the gender of the noun.

NUMBER: SINGULAR AND PLURAL Nouns and verbs are sometimes said to indicate number – either singular (i.e. one), or plural (i.e. more than one):

boat is singular   (one boat)
boats is plural   (more than one boat)
was is singular   (the subject can only be one person – *I*, *he*, *she* or *it*)
were could be singular or plural   (*you* singular, as in 'you were wrong, John', or *we*, *you*, *they*, referring to more than one person)

ADJECTIVE Words which give more information about a noun, relating to ownership, size, color, shape etc:

jacket   (no other information given)
my good old brown jacket   (adjectives tell us a lot more)

COMPARATIVE AND SUPERLATIVE Adjectives can be used to compare nouns with each other, e.g. more expensive, most expensive:

When two things are being compared the adjective is said to be a comparative:

the *more intelligent* of the two
the *quieter* one

When more than two things are being compared the adjective is said to be a superlative:

the *most intelligent* of all
the *quietest* one

ADVERB A word which gives information about verbs, describing how a process is carried out:

you work *slowly*   he paints *beautifully*   they were talking *quietly*

or gives more information about adjectives:

he is *too* old   I am *quite* amazed   I'm *very* hungry

PREPOSITION A word which is positioned in front of a noun or pronoun and normally illustrates some connection between that noun or pronoun and another idea in the sentence:

he was standing *behind* the door   (i.e. where he was standing in relationship to the door)

she was going *to* the supermarket   (i.e. where she was going in relationship to the supermarket – *to* it, not *away* from it)

he had a present *for* me   (i.e. the connection between 'me' and the 'present' is that it's intended for 'me')

NEGATIVE AND POSITIVE A negative statement has a word such as 'not', 'never', 'no more', 'no one', 'nothing', contained in it:

I saw *nothing*
I did*n't* hear a thing
I've *never* been to Switzerland

A positive statement contains *no* words of the type mentioned above:

I saw a man
I heard a car
I have been to Switzerland

AFFIRMATIVE AND INTERROGATIVE A sentence which makes a statement of fact is affirmative:

gasoline costs 4 francs per liter in France

A sentence which asks a question is interrogative:

is gasoline 4 francs per liter in France?

INTONATION The rise and fall of your voice, which can affect the meaning of what you are saying. For example, if you say: 'you've finished' with a *rising* intonation, making your voice go up at the end of the sentence, then you are asking a question (i.e., 'has the person finished?'). If you say the same words without making your voice go up at the end of the sentence, then you are simply making a statement (i.e., 'the person has finished').

FAMILIAR AND POLITE FORMS OF 'YOU' The distinction between a familiar form of the word 'you' (**tu**) and a more formal polite form of the same word (**vous**) is an important element of modern French, although this distinction no longer exists in English. The familiar form **tu** should be used when talking to one person *only* with whom there is a close relationship.

WORD ORDER AND INVERSION Word order clearly means the order in which the words of a sentence are arranged. Changing the order of words often changes the meaning radically, e.g.

the bull chased the man
the man chased the bull

Bear in mind, however, that you cannot always expect the word order to be identical in two languages. For example, in English we would say 'I'm talking to her', whereas the word order in French would be 'I'm to her talking.' A 'striped shirt' becomes a 'shirt striped' in French.

Inversion, or inverted word order occurs when the subject comes after the verb, instead of before, generally when asking a question:

you have finished your work   (normal word order)
have you finished your work?   (inverted word order)

VOWEL AND CONSONANT The letters *a e i o u y* (and often the letter *h* in French) are vowels. All other letters are said to be consonants.

IDIOM Learning a foreign language is like learning a code, but not a code where one word in one language always corresponds exactly to another word in the second language. Languages 'divide up' reality in different ways, and have their own individual style of expressing ideas, some of which sound odd when translated word for word. For example, the French say 'I have hunger' rather than 'I'm hungry', 'it makes some sunshine' rather than 'it is sunny'. Phrases such as this are said to be 'idioms', or 'idiomatic phrases'.

Grammar reference

Verbs

See under separate paragraph headings

USAGES:
- the key to understanding and speaking more complicated sentences in French
- separate paragraph headings give precise usages

INTRODUCTION This section of the book has to be long because verbs are so important. Please try to read this introduction before you tackle the different paragraphs.

Everything you wanted to know about verbs ... and didn't dare ask

It is hard to say or understand anything beyond very simple things in French without tackling verbs. However, it may well be that learning lists of verbs has discouraged you from learning French in the past!

Don't panic when you see the verb tables and explanations in this book. There are some short cuts. Things should become clearer if you read the following question-and-answer guide before launching into the sections on tenses.

1 What is a verb?
A verb denotes an action, state or event. In the following pairs of sentences the verbs are underlined.

nous <u>consultons</u> toujours la carte	we <u>are</u> still <u>looking</u> at the menu
c'<u>est</u> votre voiture, monsieur?	<u>is</u> this your car, sir?
le président <u>est mort</u>	the president <u>has died</u>

2 What is a regular verb?

One which follows a definite, predictable pattern – or in other words behaves in a regular way like large numbers of other verbs in the same type or family. A regular French verb in a verb table or dictionary will be one of three types:

Type 1: last two letters are **-er**
Type 2: last two letters are **-ir**
Type 3: last two letters are **-re**

Once you have mastered these three types of regular verbs you have thousands of verbs at your command because you can *predict* how a regular verb which is new to you will behave according to the set pattern you will have learned.

3 What is an irregular verb?

One which has its own individual pattern. This means that there's more to memorize, but make every effort to learn your irregular verbs because they are the ones that come up most frequently in everyday speech and are therefore the ones you are most likely to need.

4 Are there any short cuts or do I have to learn all those verb tables?

Cut down your work as follows:

- *Don't* simply memorize the verb tables as they stand. Even if you succeeded in reciting all of them you would not be able to communicate anything sensible or useful.

- *Do* work through the verb paragraphs (pp.17–42) which explain the uses of verbs. Any memorization you do on the verb tables will be more useful at that point because then you will see *why* you are memorizing and what you will gain from your efforts when you go abroad.

- *Do* decide on your priorities and needs. If you are happy simply to understand and are not too worried about speaking, then you need only concentrate on *recognizing* certain patterns in verbs. This is much easier than having to memorize verbs so as to be able to produce the French yourself.

- *Do* concentrate on the verbs and tenses which you think will be of most use to you. Each paragraph in this section on verbs tells you *when* and *where* the information given to you might be useful. If your time is limited, learning a few key verbs well is better than only half-knowing a larger number. Pages 36–39 on the infinitive are a possible time-saver in this respect.

- *Do* concentrate on the *persons* (*I*, *you*, *he*, *we* etc) of the verbs which you will need to use. If you are mainly interested in saying sentences beginning with 'I' or 'we', then concentrate on the **je** and **nous** parts of the verb. If you are going to be asking lots of questions, the **on** part of the verb is very useful. Only if you feel you will want to talk about other people (e.g. she has lost her passport, my son is ill) do the **il/elle** and **ils/elles** parts of the verb become important. The **tu** part of the verb which you use for 'you' when addressing someone with whom you are on familiar terms will only be relevant to your needs if you intend to be on friendly terms with someone during your visit.

- *Don't* worry if you make mistakes when speaking, you are still likely to be understood. Sorting out the differences between the tenses (which will be explained to you in the following pages) and getting them reasonably correct is probably the key to avoiding major misunderstandings.

- *Don't* get 'bogged down' in this section on verbs. Verbs are important, but they are only of any real use to you if you can use other words and items of grammar from the other sections of the book. You can either work through this section from beginning to end, or, if you have a clear idea of what your needs will be abroad, use the *Topic index* to refer you to the relevant paragraphs.

The present

TIY: p.79

USAGES: Saying
- what you are doing now
- what you do as a routine
- how you feel
- what people, places or things are like
- you've been wait ⎫
        work ⎬ ing   for . . . minutes, hours,
        etc ⎭   days, years
- what you intend to do in the immediate future

EXPLANATION: In English, the present tense can be expressed in several different ways:

I speak French   (better than I speak German)
I do speak French   (but I'm too tired, so I'll speak English)
I am speaking French   (with some difficulty because I'm a beginner)

In French there is only ONE way of saying something in the present tense:

je parle français   I speak French
                        I do speak French
                        I am speaking French

NB: the French verb **parler** is ONE word for all three meanings in English, never two words as in *do speak*, *am speaking*. In French ONE FORM, ONE WORD

You will see from the column marked *Present* in the verb tables beginning on p.125 that the present tense is formed by removing the last two letters (**-er**, **-ir** or **-re**) from regular verbs and replacing them with these letters according to the subject (*I, you, he* etc):

Type 1 **-er**		Type 2 **-ir**	Type 3 **-re**
je	-e	-is	-s
tu	-es	-is	-s
il			
elle	-e	-it	no letters added
on			
nous	-ons	-issons	-ons
vous	-ez	-issez	-ez
ils	-ent	-issent	-ent
elles			

The present tense of some very important irregular verbs is given in full in the verb tables beginning on p.127. There are many predictable patterns in these so-called irregular verbs, which makes learning them less difficult. This applies especially to their endings.

When using the **je** part of the verb, the **je** shortens to **j'** if the verb starts with a vowel (a, e, i, o, u + h, which often counts as a vowel in French):

aimer   to like, to love   **j'aime**   I like, I love

If you forget this it won't matter a great deal, but it will grate on the ear of a French person, somewhat like someone saying 'a orange' in English.

USAGES: Use the present tense to

say what you're doing now

j'attends mon mari	I'm waiting for my husband

say what you do as a routine

je prends ce médicament 4 fois par jour	I take this medicine 4 times a day

say how you feel

je suis fiévreux	I feel feverish (I have a high temperature)
je suis d'accord	I agree

say what people, places or things are like

je suis célibataire	I'm a bachelor
c'est un bel appartement	it's a nice apartment
mon fils est allergique à la pénicilline	my son is allergic to penicillin

say you've been '...ing' for ... minutes, hours, days etc, i.e. to express an activity or a state of affairs which has been going on for a period of time (and is *still* going on). **depuis** = for.

je travaille à Macy's depuis deux ans	I've been working at Macy's for two years
j'apprends le français depuis cinq ans	I've been learning French for five years
je suis malade depuis plusieurs jours	I've been ill for several days
j'attends depuis une demi-heure	I've been waiting half an hour
j'habite Boston depuis six mois	I've been living in Boston for six months

say what you intend to do in the fairly immediate future

nous partons demain matin à 9 heures	we're leaving tomorrow morning at 9 o'clock

The imperfect

TIY: p.80

USAGES: Saying
- what you used to do (e.g. when you were younger)
- what someone, some place or some thing looked like
- what you were doing but never finished

EXPLANATION: English has several ways of expressing the first two items on the usages list above:

when I was 25 . . . I used to work in Chicago
I was working in Chicago
I worked in Chicago

In French there is only ONE way of expressing the imperfect tense for all *three* usages. In these examples you will see that the imperfect tense is contained in ONE word in French, not two or three as in English 'was working', 'used to work':

quand j'avais 25 ans, je travaillais à Chicago	when I was 25, I used to work/ was working/worked in Chicago
tu le connais: il portait une veste en daim ce soir-là	you know him: he was wearing a suede jacket that night
je tournais à gauche quand il a brûlé le feu rouge	I was turning left when he went through the red light

The imperfect tense is very easy to form. Take the **nous** form of the present tense (see *Verb tables* p.125), remove the final three letters (**-ons**) and then add on the following endings:

je	-ais	nous	-ions
tu	-ais	vous	-iez
il elle on	-ait	ils elles	-aient

The only exception to this rule is the verb **être** (to be) where the endings printed above are added to the letters **ét-**

j'étais I was   **il était** he was etc

Be careful! Don't forget that the imperfect tense is contained in ONE word in French, not two, as is often the case in English:

je cherchais une caisse I was looking for a cash register

If you're not careful you might find yourself saying something like **j'étais chercher** (I was to look for), which is the sort of mistake that *will* keep your message from getting through. **J'étais** has to be followed by an adjective for it to make sense:

j'étais déçu	I was disappointed
j'étais malade	I was ill

USAGES: Use the imperfect tense to
talk about things you used to do

je travaillais comme routier quand j'habitais Cincinnati	I worked as a truck driver when I lived in Cincinnati

to describe how people, places or things looked

il était très grand et il portait une veste en cuir	he was very tall and he was wearing a leather jacket
San Francisco était une belle ville dans les années 60	San Francisco was a fine town in the 60s
les campings en Suisse étaient très propres	the campsites in Switzerland were very clean

to say how you or someone else felt

j'étais très ému	I was very excited
ma femme était épuisée	my wife was exhausted

to say what you were doing (or someone else was doing) but never finished

je prenais mon café quand . . .	I was having my coffee when . . .
l'autre voiture ralentissait quand . . .	the other car was slowing down when . . .
nous cherchions une sortie . . .	we were looking for an exit . . .

The perfect

TIY: p.81

USAGES: Saying
- what you did
- what you've done
- what has happened to you

EXPLANATION: English has several ways of expressing the items in the usages list above:

I finished my meal
I have finished my meal
I did finish my meal

In French there is only ONE way of expressing the perfect tense

j'ai fini mon repas $\left\{ \begin{array}{l} \text{I have finished} \\ \text{I finished} \\ \text{I did finish} \end{array} \right.$

Always think of the perfect tense as having TWO parts:
Part 1: **j'ai** I have (called the 'auxiliary verb', because it helps the main verb to do its job).
Part 2: **fini** finished (called the 'past participle', and often ending in '-ed' in English, e.g. arrived, departed).

Don't be misled by the English past tense into thinking you can say **je fini**: you cannot leave out the auxiliary verb (**j'ai**) in French. Remember ONE WAY, TWO PARTS.

Here are some extra points to remember about the two parts of the perfect tense.

Part 1 (the auxiliary)
The auxiliary verb is nearly always **avoir** (to have)
j'ai fini I have finished
But with the following verbs the auxiliary is **être** (to be)

aller to go	**arriver** to arrive	**entrer** to enter
venir to come	**partir** to leave	**rentrer** to get
sortir to go out	**monter** to go up	back/home
rester to stay,	**tomber** to fall	**retourner** to go back
to remain	**descendre** to go	**naître** to be born
	down	**mourir** to die

Try to memorize this short list of verbs.

The following pairs of French and English sentences are worth learning by heart:

l'année dernière nous sommes allés en Allemagne	last year we went to Germany
je suis venue le plus tôt possible	I came as soon as possible
nous sommes arrivés ce matin	we arrived this morning
ma nièce est partie en Ecosse la semaine dernière	my niece left for Scotland last week
mon fils est entré dans l'université en septembre	my son went off to college in September
nous sommes rentrés sans anicroches	we got home without any problems
mon frère est rentré à Portland	my brother has gone back to Portland
mon mari est sorti	my husband has gone out
nous sommes restés jusqu'à la fin	we stayed until the end
mon collègue est déjà monté	my colleague has already gone up
ma collègue est déjà descendue	my (female) colleague has already gone down
les jumeaux sont nés en 1950	the twins were born in 1950
mon père est mort en 1970	my father died in 1970
ma fille est tombée dans la rue	my daughter has fallen in the street

If you make a mistake with these verbs and say **j'ai ... nous avons ... il a ... ils ont ...** instead of **je suis ... nous sommes ... il est ... ils sont ...** you will probably be understood but it will grate on a French ear!

Part 2 (the past participle)

You can check on the past participle of many verbs by looking at the *Perfect* column in the verb tables beginning on p.125. But to save you the trouble of looking them up each time, try to learn the following patterns.

A Regular verbs (marked 'reg.' in a dictionary) ending in **-er**, **-ir** or **-re** are predictable. Having learned the pattern they follow, you can apply it to thousands of regular verbs.

Type 1 **-er** e.g. **donner** to give
j'ai donné I gave, have given, did give
NB: both **donner** and **donné** are pronounced in the same way, approximately 'ay' as in pay/hay in English.

Type 2 **-ir** e.g. **finir** to finish
j'ai fini I finished, have finished, did finish

Type 3 **-re** e.g. **attendre** to wait
j'ai attendu I waited, have waited, did wait

Try to memorize these three pairs of sentences:

j'ai fini mon café	I finished my coffee
j'ai donné un billet de 50 au garçon	I gave a 50 (franc) note to the waiter
j'ai attendu un taxi devant le restaurant	I waited for a taxi in front of the restaurant

B Irregular verbs (marked 'irreg.' in a dictionary) ending in **-ir** and **-re** are less predictable and have to be checked in the verb tables for their past participles and then memorized, e.g. **prendre** to take, **recevoir** to receive, **écrire** to write

j'ai pris un autobus	I took a bus
j'ai reçu cette lettre	I received this letter
j'ai écrit deux fois	I've written twice

The irregular verbs are grouped together in the verb tables in a way which shows you that there are some 'family resemblances' between certain verbs. This should make it easier for you to memorize them. e.g. **boire** (to drink) is grouped with **voir** (to see) because they both have a similar sounding past participle:

j'ai bu assez de vin I've drunk enough wine
j'ai vu ce film à la télé I've seen this film on television

Agreements

If you wish to use the perfect tense in a letter, then for accuracy you should apply the following rule:

In the case of the small number of verbs that use **être** for their auxiliary (see p.22), the past participle has to agree in *gender* and *number* with the person or subject of the sentence:

masculine singular subject: nothing is added to the past participle

feminine singular subject: **-e** is added to the past participle

masculine plural subject: **-s** is added to the past participle

feminine plural subject: **-es** is added to the past participle

il est arrivé he arrived (masculine singular)
elle est arrivée she arrived (feminine singular)
les hommes sont arrivés the men arrived (masculine plural)
les dames sont arrivées the ladies arrived (feminine plural)

When speaking, these extra letters usually make no difference in pronunciation. One exception, however, is the verb **mourir** (to die) where the **t** in the past participle is pronounced if there is an extra **-e** or **-es** added:

mon grand-père est mort my grandfather has died
(**t** is silent)

ma grand-mère est morte my grandmother has died
(**t** is pronounced)

NB: do not add any extra letters to the past participles of verbs that use **avoir** as their auxiliary.

Venir de + infinitive

TIY: p.83

USAGES: Saying
• what you have just done

EXPLANATION: If you want to say you have just done something it is possible to do so without using the perfect tense. Instead, use the verb **venir** in the present tense (see *Verb tables* p.129), followed by the word **de**, plus the infinitive of whatever verb you wish to use to say what you've just done.

1 Remember the infinitive is the verb as spelled in a word list or dictionary, ending either in the letters **-er**, **-ir** or **-re**.

2 The word **de** which you have to use in front of the infinitive will shorten to **d'** if the infinitive starts with a vowel.

je viens de téléphoner	I just telephoned
je viens d'arriver	I've just arrived
nous venons de manger	we've just eaten
nous venons d'entendre un bruit	we just heard a noise

USAGES: **Venir de** can only be used as explained above. It is an extremely handy and very easy way of talking about something you've done in the very recent past, with far fewer possibilities for mistakes than the perfect tense. Some further examples:

ma femme vient de partir	my wife has just left
mon fils vient de se marier	my son just got married
je viens de commencer un nouvel emploi	I've just started a new job
ma fille vient de lire ce livre	my daughter just read that book

The pluperfect

TIY: p.83

USAGES: Understanding
• someone talking about what he/she had done
• someone talking about what had happened

EXPLANATION: When you speak or write English you automatically choose the correct tense.

You would *not* say: I have already left the house when my friends arrived

You *would* say: I had (or I'd) already left the house when my friends arrived

French people automatically select the correct tense, too.

A French person would *not* say: **j'ai déjà quitté la maison quand mes amis sont arrivés**

A French person *would* say: **j'avais déjà quitté la maison quand mes amis sont arrivés**

As in English the auxiliary verb changes from the present tense **j'ai** (I have) to the imperfect tense **j'avais** (I had)

If the auxiliary verb is **être** then this too changes from the present tense **je suis** to the imperfect **j'étais**:

je suis sorti   I have gone out
j'étais sorti   I had gone out

Apart from this change in the tense of the auxiliary verb, the pluperfect follows all the rules already explained for the perfect tense.

USAGES: Concentrate on *understanding* the pluperfect when you hear it or see it written down. If you can use the perfect reasonably correctly, then you'll be understood even if what you are saying requires a pluperfect in French. One or two further examples:

il s'était cassé la jambe	he had broken his leg
il m'avait écrit deux jours avant	he had written to me two days earlier
j'avais déjà mis mon clignotant gauche	I had already signaled a left turn
nous avions déjà fini notre repas	we had already finished our meal

The future

TIY: p.84

USAGES: Understanding
- what will happen at some future time or date according to official information

EXPLANATION: One way of forming the future tense in English is by putting 'will' in front of the infinitive form of the verb:

tomorrow there will be scattered showers
rain will fall over the eastern half of the country
flights out of New York will be subject to delay

In French the future tense is contained in ONE word:

la pluie tombera sur la moitié est du pays	rain will fall over the eastern half of the country

This 'one word' future in French is split into two halves, however:

Part 1: the stem (which never alters)
Part 2: the ending (certain letters added to the stem which alter according to the subject, *I, you, he, we* etc)

So remember, ONE WORD SPLIT INTO TWO PARTS.

Part 1 (the stem)
The stem for regular verbs can be worked out from the infinitive, which is the way the verb is listed in a dictionary or verb table, as follows:

the stem is exactly the same as the infinitive:

Type 1 **-er** ⎰ future stem of **donner** (to give)   **donner-**
Type 2 **-ir** ⎱ future stem of **finir** (to finish)   **finir-**

Type 3 **-re**   future stem is the infinitive with the final **e** removed:
future stem of **attendre** (to wait)   **attendr-**

The stem for irregular verbs, however, is not as predictable. For irregular verbs check the *Future* column of the verb tables beginning on p.127.

e.g. **faire** to do, to make; future stem → **fer-**
pouvoir to be able; future stem → **pourr-**
avoir to have; future stem → **aur-**

Remember, the stem remains the *same*, regardless of the person or subject (*I*, *you*, *he* etc).

Part 2 (the endings)
The endings, or letters added to the stem are as follows, according to the subject of the verb:

je	-ai	nous	-ons
tu	-as	vous	-ez
il		ils	
elle	-a	elles	-ont
on			

Add the endings to the stem and you have the future tense:

vous me donnerez combien?	how much will you give me?
ils finiront quand?	when will they finish?
vous perdrez votre temps	you will be wasting your time
je ferai un petit tour	I will take (make) a little walk
il pourra venir à la réunion?	will he be able to come to the meeting?
vous aurez une petite attente	you will have a short wait

THE STEM NEVER CHANGES, THE ENDINGS DO.

Because the future tense is mainly used in official communications and notices, you will most frequently hear or see the **il/elle/on** and **ils/elles** forms. You are most likely to meet the **vous** form when reading your horoscope in a French magazine!

dans la matinée il fera beau sur toute la France	in the morning the weather will be good throughout France
quelques averses tomberont sur la côte normande	some showers will fall on the Normandy coast
la circulation sera perturbée près de l'échangeur de Senlis	traffic will be disrupted near the Senlis interchange
vous recevrez des nouvelles d'un ami	you will receive news from a friend

USAGES: Concentrate on *recognizing* this tense and understanding it. There is practically no need to use it yourself. To say what you are going to do in the fairly immediate future, use the present tense (p.17). To say what you are going to do a little further ahead in the future, use **aller** + infinitive (p.36).

The conditional

USAGES:
- understanding statements about what would happen
- saying what you would do if . . .
- saying what you would like
- asking politely about the availability or possibility of something

EXPLANATION: The four usages above correspond very largely to the way we use the conditional in English, as you will see from the following pairs of sentences:

A statements about what would happen:

vous avez dit que les photos seraient prêtes mardi	you said the photos would be ready on Tuesday
nous avons dit que nous arriverions tard dans la soirée	we said we would arrive late in the evening

B saying what you would do if . . . :

je prendrais ma retraite si je pouvais	I would retire if I could

C saying what you would like:

je voudrais une chambre à deux lits avec douche	I'd like twin beds with a shower
nous voudrions parler au patron	we'd like to speak to the manager

D asking politely about availability or possibility:

vous auriez un vin du pays?	would you (happen to) have a local wine?
vous auriez la bonté de fermer la fenêtre?	would you be so kind as to close the window?

The conditional is similar to the future tense (p.28) in the way it is formed. Follow all the rules on how to form the future, but add this different set of endings to the future stem:

je	-ais	nous	-ions
tu	-ais	vous	-iez
il elle on	-ait	ils elles	-aient

attendre to wait; future stem **attendr-** → **nous attendrions** (we would wait)

être to be; future stem **ser-** → **je serais** (I would be)

finir to finish; future stem **finir-** → **il finirait** (he would finish)

USAGES: Concentrate mainly on *recognizing* and *understanding* the conditional. Use it yourself with **je voudrais** (I would like) or **nous voudrions**, **il voudrait** etc, *either* followed by the thing you want:

je voudrais un Pernod	I'd like a Pernod
nous voudrions une chambre avec salle de bains	we'd like a room with a bathroom
ce monsieur voudrait 50 litres d'essence	this gentleman would like 50 liters of gasoline

or followed by the infinitive to say what you would like to do:

nous voudrions manger sur la terrasse	we'd like to eat on the terrace
ce couple voudrait faire un coup de téléphone	this couple would like to make a phone call
je voudrais prendre un chocolat chaud	I'd like to have a hot chocolate

In the course of conversation you can indulge in fantasies about what you would do 'if...' by using the conditional, but remember that the verb in the 'if...' part of your sentence has to go in the imperfect (p.20):

si j'étais riche, je ferais une croisière	if I were rich, I would go on a cruise
si nous étions riches, nous achèterions une résidence secondaire	if we were rich, we would buy a second home

The conditional perfect

TIY: p.86

USAGES:
● understanding newspaper, television or radio reports

EXPLANATION: The conditional perfect form of the verb is used in press, television and radio reports instead of the perfect tense in order to indicate that an event has *supposedly* happened. Instead of using the present tense of **avoir** or **être** as the auxiliary verb for the perfect tense, e.g.

le président Reagan a démissionné	President Reagan has resigned
le président Mitterand est parti pour Moscou	President Mitterand has left for Moscou

the conditional of **avoir** or **être** is used as the auxiliary:

le président Reagan aurait démissionné	President Reagan is reported to have resigned
le président Mitterand serait parti pour Moscou	President Mitterand is reported to have left for Moscow

As most reports are in the 3rd person singular or plural (*he/she/they*), **aurait/serait** and **auraient/seraient** followed by the past participle of the verb are the forms you are most likely to hear or see.

USAGES: Concentrate on *recognizing* the conditional perfect. If you see or hear something that looks or sounds like a perfect (p.22) but has **aurait/serait** or **auraient/seraient** instead of **a/est ont/sont** for the auxiliary part, then it means that the report is unconfirmed, not fact. Here are some more examples:

'je ne suis pas un assasin', aurait-il dit	'I am not a murderer', he is reported to have said
les douaniers britanniques auraient découvert la filière française	British customs officers are reported to have found the 'French connection'
Mme Thatcher serait arrivée à Dublin	Mrs Thatcher is reported to have arrived in Dublin
les envoyés du Pape seraient repartis pour le Vatican	the Pope's envoys are reported to have gone back to the Vatican

The imperative

TIY: p.86

USAGES:
● understanding and giving instructions

EXPLANATION: Being able to understand and give instructions is clearly helpful to you in the course of your visit abroad. A verb used to give an instruction is said to be an imperative. There are three broad types of imperatives – the one-word type, the phrase type and the infinitive type.

Type 1 (one-word)

Most verbs have imperative forms of the one-word type as follows:

A **regarde!** look! (an instruction issued to one person with whom you are on familiar terms and would address as **tu**)

B **regardez!** look! (an instruction issued to one person with whom you are on more formal terms *or* to more than one person regardless of your relationship)

C **regardons!** let's look! (in effect an instruction to yourself and at least one other person)

The rule for deriving the imperative form from the infinitive of regular verbs is presented below:

	-er verbs (e.g. **écouter**)	**-ir** verbs (e.g. **choisir**)	**-re** verbs (e.g. **attendre**)
A	remove **-er** add **-e** **écoute!** listen!	remove **-ir** add **-is** **choisis!** choose!	remove **-re** add **-s** **attends!** wait!
B	remove **-er** add **-ez** **écoutez!** listen!	remove **-ir** add **-issez** **choisissez!** choose!	remove **-re** add **-ez** **attendez!** wait!
C	remove **-er** add **-ons** **écoutons!** let's listen!	remove **-ir** add **-issons** **choisissons!** let's choose!	remove **-re** add **-ons** **attendons!** let's wait!

The imperative of irregular verbs is not, unfortunately, as predictable (see columns marked *Command* in the verb tables on p.127–9).

Type 2 (phrase type)

If giving instructions or making requests, it is more common to use a phrase rather than the one-word imperative:

A **veux-tu** + infinitive of a verb (when addressing one person with whom you are on familiar terms)
voulez-vous + infinitive of a verb (when addressing one person more formally or several people formally or informally)

veux-tu me passer le livre?	would you hand me the book?
voulez-vous écrire cela?	would you please write that?

B the present tense of the verb (formal or informal words for 'you' as appropriate)

tu me passes le sel s'il te plaît?	would you please pass me the salt?
vous me passez la moutarde s'il vous plaît?	would you please pass me the mustard?
vous me mettez des poires à 5.20 le kilo	put some pears at 5.20 a kilo (in this bag)
vous me mettez 100 francs de super	put 100 francs worth of gas (in the tank)

C on va + infinitive of the verb (for the instruction 'let's . . .' or 'shall we . . .?')

on va prendre un apéritif?	shall we have an aperitif?
on va signer le contrat?	shall we sign the contract?
on va prendre un autre rendez-vous?	let's set up another appointment

Type 3 (infinitive)

Written instructions on packages, in recipes, on road signs, for example, often use the infinitive form of the verb as an imperative:

ralentir!	slow down!	**garder au frais!**	keep cool!

ne pas se pencher au dehors! do not lean out!
battre les œufs! beat the eggs!
éplucher les légumes et couper en dés! peel the vegetables and dice!

USAGES: Use the *one-word type imperative* when you want to catch someone's attention in a hurry or want someone to stay on the telephone, i.e. when there isn't time to use a longer form

regarde!	look!
parlez!	go ahead (lit. 'speak!' on the phone)
ne quittez pas!	stay on! (on the phone)

use the *phrase type imperative* when you want to give an instruction or make a request somewhat more politely

voulez-vous vous asseoir?	would you like to sit down?

you will see the *infinitive imperative* on printed signs and notices

poussez!	push!	**tirez!**	pull!
attendez!	wait!	**passez!**	cross now!
frappez!	knock!		

empruntez le souterrain! use the underground passage!
allumez vos phares! headlights on!

The infinitive

TIY: p.88

USAGES:
- reducing some of the hard work involved in learning verb endings
- vastly increasing the number of useful things you can say
- individual paragraph headings give more precise information

EXPLANATION: The infinitive is the simplest form of a verb, the form in which verbs are listed in a verb table or dictionary. The three common endings (i.e. the last two letters) are **-er**, **-ir** or **-re** in French. In English the infinitive normally has the word 'to' in front of it:

acheter   to buy
choisir   to choose
attendre to wait

Since the infinitive really means 'to . . .', it is not much use on its own in a sentence, e.g. **je choisir**   I to choose

But, combined with another verb, the infinitive is very useful, e.g.

je vais choisir . . .   I'm going to choose
je veux choisir . . .   I want to choose
je dois choisir . . .   I've got to choose

If you know a handful of verbs which can be used with an infinitive, you can say thousands of correct sentences, because the infinitive stays the same regardless of the person (**je**, **tu**, **il** etc) or the tense (present, perfect etc). You need only remember to select the correct ending and tense for the verb you use with the infinitive.

USAGES: Learn the following verbs in the present tense with an infinitive and you will extend considerably your ability to communicate.

aimer   to like, to enjoy
j'aime jouer au tennis   I like to play tennis
nous aimons danser   we like to dance (dancing)

aller   to be going to, to intend to
je vais rentrer tard   I intend to come back late
nous allons prendre un panier-   we'll be taking a packed lunch
  repas

avoir envie de   to feel like (**de** always shortens to **d'** before a word beginning with a vowel)

j'ai envie de boire quelque chose	I feel like drinking something
tu as envie de manger quelque chose?	do you feel like eating something?

avoir l'intention de   to intend to

nous avons l'intention de repartir en Amérique avant le weekend	we intend to go back to America before the weekend

commencer à   to begin to

je commence à me fâcher	I'm beginning to get angry
nous commençons à avoir froid	we're beginning to feel cold

détester   to hate

je déteste attendre	I hate to wait (waiting)

devoir   to have to

je dois vous quitter maintenant	I have to leave you know
nous devons trouver un concessionaire VW	we have to find a VW dealer
on doit porter la ceinture de sécurité?	do you have to wear the safety belt?

(also useful in the conditional form **vous devriez** you ought to)

vous devriez nous rembourser	you ought to give us our money back

espérer   to hope to

j'espère vendre ma voiture	I'm hoping to sell my car
nous espérons acheter un nouvel appartement	we're hoping to buy a new apartment

s'excuser de   to be sorry for, to apologize for

je m'excuse d'être en retard	I'm sorry for being late
nous nous excusons de vous déranger	we're sorry to disturb you

falloir   to be necessary (used only in **il** form = it is necessary)

il faut prendre un panier?	do you have to take a basket?
qu'est-ce qu'il faut faire?	what do you have to do? (i.e. how does this work?)

pouvoir   to be able, to be allowed to

on peut fumer ici?	can you smoke here?
on peut sortir par ici?	can you get out this way?

où est-ce qu'on peut acheter un adapteur?	where can you buy an adapter?
vous pouvez charger l'appareil pour moi?	can you load the camera for me?
qu'est-ce qu'on peut faire dans la ville?	what can you do in the town?

préférer   to prefer to
je préfère attendre	I prefer to wait
nous préférons manger sur la terrasse	we prefer to eat on the terrace

savoir   to know how to
je sais nager	I know how to swim (I can swim)
nous ne savons pas téléphoner en Allemagne	we don't know how to phone Germany

venir de   to have just done something
je viens d'acheter cette pellicule	I've just bought this film
nous venons de tomber en panne	our car has just broken down

vouloir   to want, to wish to
je veux voir un médecin	I wish to see a doctor
nous voulons encaisser un chèque de voyage	we wish to cash a traveler's check

(Also used in the conditional form **je voudrais...**   I would like to... and **nous voudrions...**   we would like to...)

The perfect tense of these verbs, used with the infinitive form of another verb, enables you to say many more useful things:

commencer à   to begin to
j'ai commencé à m'habituer à la nourriture	I've begun to get used to the food
nous avons commencé à refaire notre appartement	we've begun to decorate our apartment

décider de   to decide to
on a décidé de prendre le menu à 35 francs	we've decided to have the 35-franc meal
j'ai décidé de sauter le dessert	I've decided to skip the dessert

essayer de   to try to
j'ai essayé d'ouvrir la porte	I've tried to open the door
nous avons essayé de vous toucher par téléphone	we tried to get in touch with you by phone

finir de   to finish doing something

j'ai fini de manger	I've finished eating
nous avons fini de consulter la carte	we've finished looking at the menu

pouvoir   to be able to/to manage to

vous avez pu réparer le pneu?	have you managed to fix the tire?
je n'ai pas pu trouver un parking	I couldn't find a parking space

Expressions with *avoir* and *faire*

TIY: p.89

USAGES:
- expressing a large number of everyday phrases, many having to do with personal feelings and reactions
- the *present* tense of these expressions is probably the most frequently used, although **avoir** and **faire** can be used in the infinitive form when coupled with another verb.

EXPLANATION: Some of the common everyday phrases in French are idiomatic and do not correspond word for word with English usage, e.g. in English, we talk about *being* frightened, while in French, you talk about *having* fear of, just as you *have* hunger (not *feel* hungry), *have* 25 years (rather than *being* 25 years old), *make* an outing (not *go on* an outing) and *do* some camping (not *go* camping).

USAGES:
avoir expressions:

avoir chaud	to feel hot
je commence à avoir chaud	I'm beginning to feel hot
avoir froid	to feel cold
ma femme a froid	my wife feels cold
avoir faim	to feel hungry
je n'ai plus faim	I'm full (no longer hungry)

avoir soif	to feel thirsty
nous avons soif	we feel thirsty
avoir raison	to be right
j'ai raison?	am I right?
avoir tort	to be wrong
vous avez tort	you're wrong
avoir __ ans	to be __ years old
mon fils a 18 ans	my son is 18
avoir peur de	to be frightened of
j'ai peur des chats	I'm frightened of cats
avoir besoin de	to need
j'ai besoin d'un médecin	I need a doctor
nous avons besoin de pain	we need bread
nous avons besoin d'essence	we need gasoline
avoir mal à	to have a pain in . . . (see p.72)
ma fille a mal au genou	my daughter's knee hurts

faire expressions:

faire du camping	to go camping
nous avons fait du camping en Espagne	we've been camping in Spain
faire une excursion	to go on a trip
nous voudrions faire une excursion en bateau	we'd like to go on a boat trip
faire une promenade	to go for a walk
où est-ce qu'on peut faire une promenade?	where can you go for a walk?
faire une remise	to offer a reduction
vous faites une remise pour les personnes de troisième âge?	do you offer a reduction for senior citizens?
faire restaurant	to serve meals
on fait restaurant ici?	do they serve meals here?
faire un séjour	to stay, to vacation
vous avez jamais fait un séjour en Autriche?	have you ever stayed in Austria?

The simple past

TIY: p.90

USAGES: Understanding
• stories in the past tense in novels, newspapers and magazines

EXPLANATION: Sometimes when reading a newspaper or magazine article you will come across a different way of expressing the past tense: the simple past. Unlike the perfect, which is in *two* parts, the simple past is expressed in *one* word:

il est arrivé hier (perfect)	he arrived yesterday
il arriva hier (simple past)	he arrived yesterday
trois terroristes ont détourné l'avion (perfect)	three terrorists hijacked the plane
trois terroristes détournèrent l'avion (simple past)	three terrorists hijacked the plane

The meaning of the simple past always corresponds to the one-word past tense in English (i.e. 'arrived', 'hijacked' and *not* 'has arrived', 'have hijacked' etc). The simple past is nearly always used in the third person singular and plural forms (*he/she/they*), so you will only need to recognize the following endings:

il/elle: *-a*, *-it* or *-ut* (for **-er**, **-ir** and **-re** verbs respectively)
ils/elles: *-èrent*, *-irent* or *-urent* (for **-er**, **-ir** and **-re** verbs respectively)

These endings are added to the stem of the verb, which for regular verbs is the infinitive with the **-er**, **-ir** or **-re** removed. For irregular verbs you will need to check the column marked *Simple Past* in the verb tables beginning on p.127.

If the verb you read in a newspaper, magazine or novel fits the description above, it must be in the simple past!

USAGES: Concentrate on recognizing this tense in your reading so that you can understand the meaning. Don't attempt to use it yourself! Some further examples:

un adolescent perdit le contrôle de son vélomoteur	a teenager lost control of his motorcycle

il ouvrit les yeux et me regarda avec surprise	he opened his eyes and looked at me in surprise
il s'assit près de moi	he sat down near to me
toutes les victimes moururent de faim	all the victims died of starvation
les soldats saisirent les studios de télévision	the soldiers seized the television studios

Negatives

TIY: p.91

USAGES: Saying
● 'not', 'never', 'no more' etc.

EXPLANATION: Negative words are essential if you need to say, for example, that you do *not* want to do something. In English a negative idea is conveyed by simply adding one word to the sentence:

I do like her dress
I do not (or don't) like her dress

In French, saying a full sentence in the negative will generally involve putting in *two* extra words. To say 'not' you need to fit in the words **ne** (shortened to **n'** before a vowel) and **pas** as in the following examples:

je suis marié	I'm married
je ne suis pas marié	I'm not married (I'm single)
nous avons réservé	we've reserved
nous n'avons pas réservé	we haven't reserved
c'est grave	it's serious
ce n'est pas grave	it's not serious
j'ai vu le feu rouge	I saw the red light
je n'ai pas vu le feu rouge	I didn't see the red light

Notice that the finite verb (i.e. the verb controlled by the subject of the sentence: **suis/avons/est/ai** in the examples) is sandwiched between the **ne** and the **pas**). This general rule applies to most pairs of negative words which you will find in the usages section on the following page.

USAGES: Use **ne . . . pas** to express the idea of 'not'

je n'aime pas le saucisson à l'ail	I don't like garlic sausage

ne . . . rien for 'nothing' or 'not anything'

je n'ai rien à declarer	I have nothing to declare
je ne veux rien manger, merci	I don't want to eat anything, thanks

ne . . . plus for 'not any more', 'no more'

je ne fume plus	I don't smoke any more
je n'ai plus d'essence	I've run out of gas
vous n'avez plus de chambres?	you don't have any more rooms?

ne . . . que for 'only'

nous n'avons que deux valises	we have only two suitcases
je n'ai que deux enfants	I only have two children

ne . . . personne for 'no one' and **ne . . . jamais** for 'never' as in the other pairs. However, **personne** and **jamais** can also be used on their own:

vous êtes allé en Espagne? non, jamais	have you been to Spain? no, never
vous avez vu quelqu'un? non, personne	did you see someone? no, no one

The definite article

TIY: p.92

USAGES:
- referring to a specific object
- the clue to a plural in speech
- official titles
- dates and 'on ____days'
- asking for a per-unit price
- generalizing, especially likes and dislikes

EXPLANATION: Nouns (apart from proper nouns) have different words for 'the' in front of them; think of these as labels.

Le in front of a word tells you the gender is masculine:
le frère   the brother

La in front of a word tells you the gender is feminine:
la sœur   the sister

In French, objects can also be masculine or feminine:
le piano   the piano (masc.)   **la guitare**   the guitar (fem.)
There's no logic behind the gender of objects. You just have to learn the gender of each noun when you first come across it. If you get the word for 'the' wrong (saying **le** instead of **la** or vice versa) it won't keep your message from getting through.

If the word starts with a vowel $(a, e, i, o, u, y + h$ fairly frequently in French) both **le** and **la** shorten to **l'**:
l'ami   the friend (masculine)
l'auto   the car (feminine)

If you were to say **le ami** instead of **l'ami** it would grate on the ear of the person listening to you, just as it would on yours if a foreign speaker asked you for 'a apple' instead of 'an apple'.

Les in front of a word tells you the word is plural:
les garçons   the boys   **les filles**   the girls
You need to listen for this clue to the plural because the -s on the end of the noun is not pronounced in French.

passe-moi le verre   pass me the glass
passe-moi les verres   pass me the glasses

NB: if the noun starts with a vowel, the **s** on the end of **les** is pronounced as though it were a **z**.

USAGES: Use the definite article to
refer to a specific object

tu me passes les ciseaux	hand me the scissors
tu me passes le livre	hand me the book
pourriez-vous vérifier la batterie?	could you check the battery?
où sont les boissons non-alcoolisées?	where are the soft drinks?

refer to an official title

Monsieur le Maire	Mr. Mayor
Madame la Présidente	Madam Chairman

give the date

le vendredi 18 juin   Friday, June 18th

NB: the different word order above and no 'th' after the number as in English '18th'.

le 18 août   (on) the 18th of August

NB: no word for 'on' in French before the date.

refer to particular days

le mardi	on Tuesdays
le mercredi	on Wednesdays

NB: if you leave out **le** the meaning changes to 'on Tuesday', 'on Wednesday', i.e. this coming Tuesday or Wednesday

je peux venir le jeudi	I can come on Thursdays
je peux venir jeudi	I can come on Thursday

refer to the price of something per unit

c'est combien le kilo?	how much is it per kilo?
c'est combien la bouteille?	how much is it per bottle?
c'est combien les cent grammes?	how much is it per 100 grams?

generalize (unlike English)

j'aime les frites	I like French fries
je déteste le fromage	I hate cheese
l'essence est chère en France	gasoline is expensive in France
vous faites les réparations?	do you do repairs?

The indefinite article

TIY: p.94

USAGES: Saying
● 'a', 'an', 'some' + noun

EXPLANATION: Singular nouns can have two different words which both mean 'a' or 'an' in front of them; think of these as labels (see *The definite article*, p.43):

un in front of a noun tells you the gender is masculine
un ami   a male friend
une in front of a word tells you the gender is feminine
une amie   a female friend

In French, objects also have genders:
un piano   a piano (masc.)   **une guitare**   a guitar (fem.)
There's no logic behind the gender of objects. You have to learn the gender when you first come across the particular noun. If you say the wrong word for a/an (e.g. **un** instead of **une** or vice versa) it won't keep your message from getting through.

Dealing with plural nouns is straightforward. In English you cannot say a/an + a plural, e.g. a cars, an apples. You must either drop the a/an or replace it with the word 'some': cars, apples, some cars, some apples

In French you must *always* put in the word for 'some' in front of a plural noun. The word is **des**. The final -**s** is not pronounced, unless the following noun starts with a vowel, in which case the s is pronounced like a **z**:

des voitures   cars, some cars
des pommes   apples, some apples
des oranges   oranges, some oranges

USAGES: Use the indefinite article in French just as you would in English:

j'ai un fils et une fille	I have a son and a daughter
je voudrais une carte postale	I'd like a postcard
vous avez un plan de la ville?	do you have a map of the town?
une bière pression, s'il vous plaît	a draft beer, please
vous m'apportez un bifteck bien cuit, s'il vous plaît	bring me a steak well-done, please

NB: the word for 'a' will not appear on the menu or drinks list, so you will have to guess the gender of the item you are ordering and then select the appropriate form for 'a'.

You must, however, remember to leave out the word for 'a' when stating your or someone else's job:

je suis receveur d'autobus	I'm a bus conductor
elle est sage-femme	she's a midwife

Use **des** in front of a plural noun where you would use the word 'some' or 'any' in English:

je prends des frites	I'll have some French fries
j'ai des amis là-bas	I've got some friends in that area
vous avez des enfants?	do you have any children?

NB: remember that 'some' and 'any' can be left out in English, but apart from the one exception above, never in French.

qu'est-ce que je vous sers?	which would you like?
des petits pois ou des haricots verts?	peas or green beans?

The partitive

TIY: p.96

USAGES: Saying
• 'some' or 'any' – particularly when ordering a portion of something

EXPLANATION: If you have already looked at the section on *The indefinite article* (pp.46–7) you will know that when 'some' or 'any' refers to more than one item, e.g. some loaves of bread, any tomatoes, then in French you use **des**:

nous voudrions des grands pains   we'd like some large loaves of
                                      bread
vous avez des tomates?   do you have any tomatoes?

Use **des** whenever you can actually count the number of whole items. But, when 'some' refers to either part of a whole item or an unspecified quantity, e.g. some bread, some tomato, use one of the following:

1 **du** 'some' before a masculine word
du vin some wine   **du poivre** some pepper

2 **de la** 'some' before a feminine word
de la tomate some tomato   **de la crème** some cream

3 **de l'** 'some' before masculine and feminine words beginning with a vowel
de l'eau some water   **de l'huile** some oil
de l'aspirine some aspirin

USAGES: Use **du, de la** and **de l'**
to inquire if something is available
vous avez de la place?   do you have any room?
il y a du fromage?   is there any cheese?

to find out where you might get something
où puis-je trouver de la limonade? where can I find some lemonade?

to state what you want to buy or order

de l'agneau pour trois personnes	some lamb for three people
de la viande hachée pour deux personnes	some mincemeat for two people
je voudrais bien prendre de la glace	I'd very much like to have some ice cream

1 'some/any' could be left out in English in the sentences above (do you have room? I'd like ice cream). It *cannot* be left out in French.

2 if your sentence is in the negative, the word for 'any' is always **de** (or **d'** before a noun starting with a vowel) regardless of whether the noun is masculine, feminine, singular or plural:

nous n'avons pas de gaz	we have no gas
vous n'avez pas de crème?	don't you have any cream?
je n'ai plus d'essence	I've run out of gas
je n'ai plus de chambres	I have no more rooms
il n'y a pas de bonde dans le lavabo	there's no plug in the sink
il n'y a pas de papier hygiénique dans le w.c.	there's no paper in the toilet
il n'y a pas d'ampoule dans la lampe	there's no bulb in the lamp

So remember, to say 'not any' or 'no' + noun and 'no more'..., use **ne ... pas** (see p.42) and **plus de** or **d'**.

Expressions of quantity

TIY: p.98

USAGES: Saying
• how much you want when you are shopping (e.g. 2 liters)

EXPLANATION: Asking for a particular quantity of something is similar to English usage in many ways:

un kilo one kilo
trois kilos three kilos
un litre one liter
cinquante litres fifty liters
(Don't forget the final **-s** on **kilos** and **litres** isn't pronounced in French, though.)

The word for 'one' **un** changes to **une** if the 'quantity word' is feminine, e.g.

une tranche de tarte à l'oignon one slice of onion pie
une boîte de thé one box of tea
une paire de sandales one pair of sandals

The word for 'half a . . .' is **un** or **une demi- . . .**
un demi-kilo a half kilo
une demi-bouteille a half bottle

'One and a half' is **un . . . et demi** or **une . . . et demie**
un kilo et demi de pommes de terre a kilo and a half of potatoes
une livre et demie de beurre a pound and a half of butter

There are many other expressions of quantity:

200 francs de	200 francs worth of
un verre de	a glass of
un paquet de	a package of
une boîte de	a box or can of
une tasse de	a cup of
un pot de	a pot of or jar of
un peu de	a little (of)
trop de	too much
beaucoup de	a lot of

Notice how the word for 'of' with all the expressions of quantity listed opposite is **de** (or **d'** before a vowel):
un litre de vin   one liter of wine
un litre d'eau minérale   one liter of mineral water

USAGES: Specifying the amount you want to buy, commenting on or complaining about the amount you have been given.

vous me mettez un kilo de poires	put one kilo of pears (in my bag)
45 litres d'essence, s'il vous plaît	45 liters of gas, please
300 francs de super, s'il vous plaît	300 francs worth of super, please
trois tasses de thé au lait	three cups of tea with milk
un tube d'aspirines	a tube of aspirin tablets
un pot de confiture à la fraise	a jar of strawberry jam
un peu de sauce	a little sauce
vous m'avez servi trop d'asperges	you've served me too much asparagus
j'ai assez de vin, merci	I have enough wine, thanks

Pronouns

TIY: p.99

USAGES:
• important for *understanding* both speech and writing
• help you use fewer words and make you sound more natural when speaking French

EXPLANATION: Pronouns are bound to occur frequently in speech and writing, and it therefore helps if you can recognize them and understand their meaning. If you can use pronouns yourself, you will avoid repetition, e.g. 'is your tank empty?'/'no, *it*'s half full' sounds more natural and is shorter than 'is your tank empty?'/'no, my tank is half full'

Pronouns are complicated, however, and it will probably take you some time to get the hang of them. In the sections that follow, the main types of pronouns are explained, together with their usages.

A Subject pronouns
Some of these correspond exactly with English:

je (shortened to **j'** before a word starting with a vowel) = I

il = he   **elle** = she   **nous** = we

but others differ as follows:

1 there are *two* words for 'you'

tu = you when the person being addressed is someone with whom you have a fairly informal relationship, e.g. a friend, close colleague, young child. If in doubt about when to start saying **tu** to someone you have met, let him or her take the initiative. That way there is no risk of causing offense.

vous = you either when one person is being addressed with whom you have a more formal, distant relationship OR when more than one person is being addressed, regardless of whether the relationship is formal or informal.

2 **il** and **elle** can also mean 'it' (as well as 'he' and 'she') when standing for a noun, since objects as well as persons have genders in French:

il = 'it' when replacing a masculine noun

elle = 'it' when replacing a feminine noun

When listening to French, don't forget that **il** or **elle** might mean 'it', not 'he' or 'she', e.g. **c'est une photo de votre fille? elle est récente?** does *not* mean is this a photo of your daughter? Is *she* recent? but rather is this a photo of your daughter? Is *it* recent? since the word **elle** is replacing the feminine noun **une photo**.

3 **on** is a subject pronoun which corresponds roughly to English 'one' (as in 'one finds it hot in St Tropez in August') but it's used much more often in French – and without sounding as stilted! Any verb which has **on** as its subject will behave in exactly the same way as far as all its endings are concerned as if its subjects were **il** or **elle**, so there are no new endings to learn. **on** can also mean 'they', 'people', 'someone':

on parle anglais ici   they speak English here, people speak English here, English is spoken here

on a coupé le gaz	someone has cut the gas off, the gas has been cut off

on is also useful because in speech you can nearly always use it instead of the **nous** form of the verb, which effectively gives you fewer verb endings to learn:

on peut stationner ici?	may we park here?
on doit faire la queue ici?	do we have to line up here?
on a décidé de rester encore deux nuits	we've decided to stay another two nights

4 there are two words for 'they', **ils** and **elles**
ils replaces a masculine plural noun:

vous cherchez vos amis? ils sont là-bas	are you looking for your (male) friends? they're over there

elles replaces a feminine plural noun:

vous cherchez vos amies? elles sont là-bas	are you looking for your (female) friends? they're over there

If 'they' stands for a mixed group of males and females, e.g. a married couple or a group of boys and girls, then you must always use **ils**.

Since objects have genders too in French, **ils** and **elles** replace nouns according to whether they are masculine or feminine:

j'ai perdu mes gants: ils sont verts	I've lost my gloves: they're green

ils replaces **gants** which is masculine plural

j'ai perdu les clés: elles sont sur un porte-clés Renault	I've lost my keys: they're on a Renault keyring

elles replaces **clés** which is feminine plural.

USAGES: Subject pronouns serve the same purpose in French and English (saying 'I', 'you', 'we' etc) but as you probably have seen, the usages differ. The verb which follows these subject pronouns changes its endings according to the subject, as you will see from the verb tables beginning on p.125. To save yourself time and effort, decide before you go to a French-speaking country how ambitious you are going to be. As a bare minimum you would probably get away with using **je** and **on** as long as you can *understand* the other pronouns. However, if you want to help others who are struggling with their French, you should try to use the **il/elle** (he/she) and **ils/elles** (they) forms:

il voudrait un ballon pour la plage	he would like a beachball
elle voudrait une pellicule couleur	she'd like a roll of color film
ce couple – où peuvent-ils trouver un pharmacien?	where can this couple find a pharmacist?
ces dames sont en difficulté – elles viennent de tomber en panne	these ladies are in trouble – their car has just broken down

You would only really need to use the **tu** form if you intend to get on fairly close terms with someone. **On** will often save you from having to use the **nous**(we) and **vous**(you) forms:

on peut camper ici?	may we camp here?
on fait les réparations ici?	do they do repairs here?
	do you do repairs here?
	are repairs done here?

B Object pronouns

If you've just read the section on subject pronouns you have seen that these pronouns stand for someone or something which is performing some action or is in a particular state:

they kick the ball (they are performing the action of kicking)
he is speaking French (he is performing the action of speaking French)
I am American (I am in the state of American nationality)

These same three pronouns (*they*, *he*, *I*) cannot be used for a different purpose, for example at the end of these three sentences:

I see *they*   we see *he*   they hit *I*

Here the pronoun stands for someone on the receiving end of an action (or the object of the action) not for someone on the performing end (or the subject of the action).

In French, as in English, object pronouns can differ from the corresponding subject pronouns, as the table on the following page shows:

subject pronouns	object pronouns
je (I)	**me** (me)
tu (you)	**te** (you)
nous (we)	**nous** (us)
vous (you)	**vous** (you)
il (he or it)	**le** (him or it)
elle (she or it)	**la** (her or it)
ils (they)	**les** (them)
elles (they)	**les** (them)

Examples:

vous pouvez me donner un prix?	can you give me a price (an estimate)?
je ne vous comprends pas	I don't understand you
je la prends	I'll take it (e.g. **la chambre** (fem.) the hotel room)
je les prends	I'll take them (e.g. **les souliers** (pl.) the shoes)

In the table above, the object pronouns above the dotted line also mean *to me, to you, to us*:

je voudrais vous parler	I'd like to talk to you
vous voulez me parler?	do you wish to speak to me?

If you want to say to him, to her, to them, use:

lui = to him or to her	**leur** = to them

je dois lui montrer mon passeport?	do I have to show my passport to him? (or to her)
je leur ai écrit en avril	I wrote to them in April

USAGES: Object pronouns in French have the same function as those in English, but note the following points of difference:

1 object pronouns do not necessarily fit into the word order of the sentence that you might expect. As a general rule the object pronoun will come immediately before the finite verb, i.e. the one which is controlled by the subject of the sentence
je le vois I see him
je les ai vus I saw them

If there is an infinitive in the sentence, then the object pronoun will come in front of that infinitive

je voudrais les voir	I'd like to see them
j'ai l'intention de lui parler	I intend to talk to him

2 **me**, **te**, **le** and **la** shorten to **m'**, **t'** and **l'** before a vowel

je ne l'aime pas	I don't like it
je l'ai perdu	I've lost it
il m'a vu	he saw me

C Emphatic pronouns

The pronouns 'me', 'you' (familiar form), 'him' and 'them' have a special form when used after the following words or phrases:

pour for   **avec** with   **sans** without

chez... at or to the abode belonging to..., i.e. at my place, to my place, at your place, to your place

c'est à... *either* it belongs to me, you, etc *or* it's my, your, etc turn, the turn has come around to me, to you, etc. e.g.

ça, c'est pour moi	that's for me
on va chez toi?	shall we go to your place?
ne partez pas sans lui!	don't go without him
je vais avec lui	I'm going with him
c'est à eux	it belongs to them (or it's their turn)

NB: **elle**, **vous**, **nous** and **elles** can also be used with the words and phrases above, in which case they would mean 'her', 'you', 'us' and 'them', respectively:

chez elle	at (or to) her place
avec elle	with her
c'est pour vous	that's for you
c'est à nous	that belongs to us (or it's our turn)
pour elles	for them (referring to females)

USAGES: Finding out if, or saying that,
something belongs to someone

c'est à vous?	is that yours?
c'est à nous	that's ours

it's someone's turn in a line

c'est à vous?	is it your turn?
c'est à moi	it's my turn

Explaining that you're offering someone a tip

c'est pour vous, mademoiselle	it's for you, miss

Talking about back home in America, and referring to someone's home

chez vous, vous avez un grand jardin?	at home, do you have a big yard?
chez nous les cafés ferment à onze heures	back home the bars close at eleven

D En

A word frequently used as a pronoun in French and one you will generally hear used with a number. Depending on the context, it can mean any of the following: 'some', 'of it', 'of them', 'any' but you will often find that there is no direct English translation – as some of these examples show:

vous en voulez combien?	how much do you want? (of it, of them, of this etc)
je n'en veux pas, merci	I don't want any, thanks
j'en prends une douzaine	I'll take a dozen (of them)
tu as des frères? non, je n'en ai pas	do you have any brothers? no, I don't have any

USAGES: If you just want to be understood, there is no particular need for you to use the word **en**. If you omit it, the meaning will still be quite clear. As long as you are aware of **en**, you will not be thrown when you hear it and misunderstand the rest of the sentence because of it.

E Reflexive pronouns

Occasionally you will come across a verb in a dictionary or word list which is printed with **se** or **s'** in front of it. This **se** (or **s'** before a verb beginning with a vowel) is a reflexive pronoun, which gets its name because it 'reflects' back on to the subject of the sentence, e.g. **se laver** to wash yourself rather than wash the car or wash the dishes. The **se** part of the verb can alter according to the subject of the sentence, as you will see from the following examples:

je me lave	I wash myself
tu te laves	you wash yourselves
il/elle se lave	he/she washes himself/herself
nous nous lavons	we wash ourselves
vous vous lavez	you wash yourselves
ils/elles se lavent	they wash themselves

NB: **me**, **te** and **se** shorten to **m'**, **t'** and **s'** before a word beginning with a vowel.

The reflexive pronoun has to come immediately before the finite verb,

d'habitude je me couche à 11.30   normally I go to bed at 11:30

unless there is an infinitive in the sentence, in which case it goes before the infinitive

je vais me lever à 7.00   I'm going to get up at 7:00

If you want to use a reflexive verb in the past tense the reflexive pronoun still goes in front of the finite verb, which is always the auxiliary verb **être**:

je me suis levé à 6.00 ce matin   I got up at 6:00 this morning
nous nous sommes couchés à   we went to bed at 12:00 last night
12.00 hier soir

There are very few reflexive verbs which you are going to need to use beyond these half dozen common ones:

se réveiller	to wake up	**se lever**	to get/stand up
se laver	to wash up	**se raser**	to shave
se reposer	to have a rest	**se coucher**	to go to bed

USAGES: Concentrate on *recognizing* reflexive pronouns when used with the verbs listed. A mistake on your part is unlikely to have disastrous consequences. You are most likely to use them when talking in the present tense about your daily routine, in the past tense when describing exactly what you did on a particular day and in sentences with an infinitive:

je me lève tard le dimanche	I get up late on Sundays
on s'est couché tôt ce soir-là	we went to bed early that evening
je voudrais me reposer	I'd like to have a rest
je viens de me lever	I just got up
je dois me raser	I have to shave
où est-ce qu'on peut se laver?	where can you wash up?

Pronouns are difficult to use correctly. Even a basic explanation such as this looks very complicated. In general, concentrate on trying to understand the meaning of sentences where pronouns appear. If you do try to use sentences with reflexive pronouns, don't worry if you seem to get things wrong at first. Only practice makes for reasonable fluency. Perfection takes a lot longer!

Adjectives

TIY: p.100

USAGES: Describing
● people, places, things (e.g. lost property)

EXPLANATION: Adjectives in French differ from English adjectives in two ways, the first of which is the most important.

1 More often than not the adjective comes *after* the noun in French, while in English it comes in front
a green book **un livre vert** (lit. a book green)
a gray shirt **une chemise grise** (lit. a shirt gray)

If in doubt, always put the adjective after the noun in French, although there are a few very common adjectives which go in front, as in English

un bon repas   a good meal
un grand café   a large coffee
un petit express   a small espresso coffee
un mauvais goût   a bad (nasty) taste (flavor)
un long voyage   a long journey

2 There is a change in the spelling of the adjective according to the gender (masculine or feminine) and the number (singular or plural) of the noun. If you wish to write correctly, the following summarizes the rule about spelling:

a) for a masculine singular noun, nothing extra is added to the adjective: **un livre vert**

b) for a feminine singular noun an extra **-e** is added, unless the adjective already ends in an **-e**: **une chemise verte**

c) for a masculine plural noun, an extra **-s** is added unless the adjective already ends in **-s**: **des livres verts**

d) for a feminine plural noun, an extra **-es** is added to the adjective: **des chemises vertes**

In practice this has little effect on speech, although again if you wish to be accurate you would need to bear in mind that adding an extra **-e** or **-es** to any adjective ending in **-s** or **-t** would alter its pronunciation

un livre intéressant (**t** not pronounced)   an interesting book
une pièce intéressante (**t** pronounced)   an interesting play

NB:

1 one common adjective adds an extra **n** as well as an **-e** when describing a feminine noun

un bon restaurant   a good restaurant
une bonne pâtisserie   a good patisserie

2 another adjective adds a letter **h** as well as an **-e** when describing a feminine noun

un pullover blanc   a white sweater
une chemise blanche   a white shirt

3 when describing the material of which something is made there seems to be a lack of words like 'wooden' in French; this is made up for by saying 'of wood'

une boîte en bois   a wooden box (box of wood)
un imper en plastique   a plastic raincoat

USAGES: Use adjectives to describe

lost property

j'ai perdu . . .	I've lost . . .
un portefeuille noir	a black wallet
une petite valise en cuir	a small leather suitcase

stolen property

on m'a volé . . .	someone has stolen . . .
ma voiture, une Fiesta rouge immatriculée ODB 756X	my car, a red Fiesta with the license plate number ODB 756X
ma montre – avec un bracelet en cuir marron	a watch – with a brown leather strap

Family, friends, people you've met, places you've been to

un grand homme aux cheveux noirs	a tall man with black hair
tu te rappelles? il portait une veste en daim et un pantalon en toile	do you remember? he was wearing a suede jacket and denim trousers
le petit garçon qui s'est égaré porte une culotte verte et un t-shirt bleu	the little boy who's lost is wearing green shorts and a blue teeshirt
Pittsburgh est une ville industrielle	Pittsburgh is an industrial town
Boston est une ville très pittoresque	Boston is a very picturesque town
nous avons trouvé ce café trop bruyant	we found this café too noisy

The size or type of item you require

une petite bière	a small beer
une grande bière	a large beer
une chambre à prix moyen	an average priced room
vous avez quelque chose en coton?	do you have something in cotton?
vous avez quelque chose en plastique?	do you have something in plastic?

Possessives

TIY: p.103

USAGES: Saying
● my, your, his, her, our, their

EXPLANATION: Possessives do the same job in French as in English –
they show who owns a particular thing:

ma voiture   my car   **votre voiture**   your car

However, you will see from the table below that in French there is
more than one word which corresponds to the single words in English,
my, your, his etc.

my	**mon** or **ma** or **mes**
your (when referring to a close friend)	**ton** or **ta** or **tes**
his and her	**son** or **sa** or **ses**
our	**notre** or **nos**
your (when referring to someone more formally)	**votre** or **vos**
their	**leur** or **leurs**

Don't be alarmed by this table, remember that:

1 you will most likely only be using 'my' and 'our' when speaking.

2 if you should use the wrong word for 'my' in a sentence (e.g. saying **ma**
when it should be **mon**), the meaning of what you are saying will not be
affected.

If you are eager to speak correctly, then you must select the correct
form of each possessive on the following basis: a) according to the
gender of the noun concerned (*not* the gender of the owner of the
object) and b) the number (singular or plural) of the noun concerned
(*not* the number of the owner of the article). Once you know the
gender and the number, you can select the correct possessive:

MY   **mon** before a masculine singular noun (e.g. **le chapeau**)
           mon chapeau   my hat
           mon before any singular feminine nouns which begin with a
               vowel (e.g. **une amie**)
           mon amie   my girlfriend
           ma before a feminine singular vowel beginning with a con-
               sonant (e.g. **la voiture**)
           ma voiture   my car
           mes before any plural noun (e.g. **les bijoux**)
           mes bijoux   my jewels

The words for 'your' (referring to a friend) and 'his' and 'her' follow
exactly the same rule as for 'my' above:

YOUR   **ton chapeau**   your hat   **ton amie**   your girlfriend
           ta voiture   your car
           tes bijoux   your jewels

HIS and   **son** chapeau   his hat or her hat
HER   **son** amie   his girlfriend or her girlfriend
           etc.

The words for 'our', 'your' (referring to someone more formally) and
'their' change only according to the number of the noun and are not
affected by a change in gender:

OUR   **notre** before any singular noun
           notre appartement   our apartment
           nos before any plural noun
           nos billets   our tickets

YOUR   **votre** before any singular noun
           votre passeport   your passport
           vos billets, s'il vous plaît   your tickets, please

THEIR   **leur** before any singular noun
           leur chambre   their room
           leurs (with no change in pronunciation) before any plural
               noun
           leurs valises   their suitcases

NB: to say it's yours, it's theirs etc, see p.74.

USAGES: Use possessives in French just as you would use 'my', 'your', 'his' etc in English

c'est mon assurance	this is my insurance certificate
ce sont mes lunettes	these are my glasses
c'est votre voiture, monsieur?	is this your car, sir?
j'ai perdu mes verres de contact	I've lost my contact lenses
ce monsieur a perdu son permis de conduire	this gentleman has lost his driver's license
on m'a volé mon appareil-photo	someone has stolen my camera
c'est une photo de votre fils?	is this a picture of your son?
mon film est coincé	my film is jammed
j'ai cassé mon dentier	I've broken my dentures

Demonstratives

TIY: p.104

USAGES: Saying
• clearly which item you want when offered several

EXPLANATION: Often you need to make a choice between a number of items offered to you by saying you would like this one or that one, these or those, i.e. the one(s) nearer to you or further away from you. A demonstrative is like a label attached to the noun which demonstrates or shows what you have chosen.

These demonstratives are double labels: part of the label comes in front of the noun and has to indicate whether the noun is masculine or feminine, singular or plural; the second part of the label comes after the noun and indicates whether you mean 'this/these' or 'that/those'.

To get the first part of the label correct you need to know whether the noun is masculine or feminine and if it's singular. You have a 50-50 chance of being right and an incorrect guess won't be disastrous. Once you know or have guessed the gender, the label changes as follows:

THIS and   **ce** before a masculine noun beginning with a consonant
THAT   **ce chapeau**   this/that hat
            ce plan   this/that plan

            cet before a masculine noun beginning with a vowel
            cet adapteur   this/that adaptor
            cet ouvre-boîte   this/that can opener

            cette before any feminine noun
            cette assiette   this/that plate
            cette carte   this/that map

If the noun is plural, then the first part of the label is always **ces**:

THESE and   **ces cigarettes**   these/those cigarettes
THOSE   **ces lunettes de soleil**   these/those sunglasses
            ces aspirines   these/those aspirin

The second part of the label which comes *after* the noun shows whether you mean this or that, these or those: **-ci** = this or these
-là = that or those
ce plan-ci   this plan   **ce plan-là**   that plan
cet adapteur-ci   this adaptor
cet adapteur-là   that adaptor
ces lames de rasoir-ci   these razor blades
ces lames de rasoir-là   those razor blades
ces serviettes périodiques-ci   these sanitary napkins
ces serviettes périodiques-là   those sanitary napkins

USAGES: To indicate your choice when shopping
je prends cette ceinture-ci   I'll take this belt
je préfère ce démaquillant-là   I prefer that make-up remover

And wherever you would use 'this', 'that' etc in English:

je voudrais ce numéro-ci en   I'd like this (phone) number in
   Angleterre   England
je n'aime pas ces nu-pieds-ci   I don't like these beach shoes

NB: if you don't know the word for the object of your choice, then simply point and say **ça** which can mean 'this' or 'that'.
je voudrais ça   I'd like that
je vais prendre ça   I'll take that
j'ai besoin de ça   I need that
un gâteau comme ça   a cake like that

Comparative and superlative

TIY: p.104

USAGES: Saying
- what you are choosing or prefer
- and comparing one thing or one person with another

EXPLANATION: In French, to say '-er' or 'more', e.g. bigger, more interesting, you put the word **plus** in front of the adjective:

plus grand   bigger
plus intéressant   more interesting

There is no equivalent in French to the '-er' ending in English (taller, smaller) with one important exception which is worth remembering, **meilleur** (better):

ce vin est meilleur   this wine is better

To say 'less...', e.g. less large, less interesting, you put the word **moins** in front of the adjective:

moins grand   less big, less tall
moins intéressant   less interesting

To say 'the most...' or 'the ...-est', e.g. the most economical, the greatest, use **le plus...** in front of the adjective.

le plus grand   the largest, the tallest
le plus intéressant   the most interesting

But, the word for 'the' must change according to the gender and number of the noun, and the adjective takes on extra letters (see p.60). For reference the pattern is:

masculine singular	**le paquet le plus petit**	the smallest package
feminine singular	**la bouteille la plus petite**	the smallest bottle
masculine plural	**les paquets les plus petits**	the smallest packages
feminine plural	**les bouteilles les plus petites**	the smallest bottles

The pattern on the previous page is identical for the phrase 'the least . . .' but with the word **moins** replacing the word **plus**, i.e. **le moins cher, la moins chère, les moins chers, les moins chères** being the various forms of 'the least expensive'.

Remember, the basic formula is **le plus** + adjective for 'the most' or 'the . . .-est' and **le moins** + adjective for 'the least'.

USAGES:

To say what size or price product you require compared with one you've been offered

vous avez quelque chose de moins cher?	do you have something less expensive?
vous avez quelque chose de plus grand?	do you have something larger?
vous avez quelque chose de plus petit?	do you have something smaller?

To state your choice when offered two or more products

je prends le plus cher	I'll take the more expensive one (or 'most expensive' if more than two offered)
nous prenons le plus sec	we'll take the drier one (or 'driest one' if more than two wines offered)

To find out which of several products is most expensive, cheapest etc.

quel est le moins cher?	which is the least expensive?
quel est le plus cher?	which is the most expensive?

To find out which is the quickest, shortest, nearest etc.

quel est le train le plus rapide?	which is the quickest train?
quel est le garage le plus proche?	which is the nearest garage?
quel est le chemin le plus court?	which is the quickest way?
quel est le vin le plus doux?	which is the sweetest wine?

Talking about the youngest, oldest etc. in your family

c'est le plus âgé	that's the oldest boy
c'est la plus âgée	that's the oldest girl
ce sont les plus jeunes	these are the youngest

Adverbs

TIY: p.106

USAGES: Describing

● how an action was performed, e.g. slowly, quickly, well, badly in greater detail, e.g. played *well*, ran *slowly*

EXPLANATION: Adverbs are useful if you want to describe how some action is, or was, performed, or how some process is, or was, going: things are going well; things went badly.

You will, however, hear far more adverbs in French than you are likely to use yourself. If you hear the ending **-ment** tacked on to an adjective, this is a cue that an adverb is being used:

rapide	rapid, fast	**rapidement**	rapidly, quickly
absolu	absolute	**absolument**	absolutely
heureux	fortunate	**heureusement**	fortunately
malheureux	unfortunate	**malheureusement**	unfortunately

The two adverbs you are most likely to use are:
bien well   **mal** badly

Adverbs can also be used to give an extra shade of meaning to another adjective (or adverb):

très dangereux	very dangerous	**assez grand**	fairly large
tout près	very near	**très mal**	very badly
très bien	very well		

USAGES: Saying, or making inquiries about, how something has gone, is going etc.

le voyage s'est bien passé?	the trip went well?
ah oui, très bien	oh yes, very well
ah non, très mal	oh no, very badly
très rapidement	very quickly
très lentement	very slowly
ça va bien?	are you OK? (it goes well?)
oui, ça va bien merci, et vous?	yes, fine thanks, and you?
ça va mal	I'm not so well (it goes badly)

The word 'every'

TIY: p.106

USAGES: To say or find out
● how often something takes place

EXPLANATION: The adjective **tout** in French is one you will hear and read frequently. Used with a singular noun it will mean either 'all' or 'the whole':

tout le temps   all the time, the whole time
ouvert toute la saison   open all season, the whole season
NB: the extra **-e** on the end of **tout** when in front of a feminine noun which causes the **t** to be pronounced.

Used in front of a plural noun (with a different spelling for masculine and feminine), the meaning is 'every'

ce train circule tous les jours (often abbreviated to **t.l.j.**)	this trains runs every day (all the days)
toutes les semaines (**semaine** is feminine)	every week

Listen for **tous** or **toutes** when you are being told about the frequency of a service, for instance:

toutes les deux heures	every two hours
toutes les vingt minutes	every twenty minutes
tous les trois ans	every three years
tous les quarts d'heure	every quarter of an hour

USAGES: Use **tout** and all its forms
to find out how often something takes place

il y a un autobus tous les combien? how often is there a bus?

to understand the reply to such inquiries

toutes les cinq minutes   every five minutes

to give information when asked about frequency

je prends ce médicament toutes les quatre heures	I take this medicine every four hours
nous allons à l'étranger tous les ans	we go abroad every year

Prepositions

TIY: p.107

USAGES: Saying and understanding words like
- 'in', 'on', 'under', 'beside' etc (i.e. location)
- 'by', 'for', 'with', 'without'

EXPLANATION: Certain prepositions in French can be easily learned from a phrasebook, since they correspond broadly to the way we use prepositions in English, e.g. **sur** on, **sous** under, **dans** in
sur la table   on the table   **sous la chaise**   under the chair
dans la valise   in the suitcase

Unfortunately, the two languages do not always correspond so neatly. If you compare the following pairs of sentences and phrases you will see that in French the preposition is *either* a) different from what you would expect in your own language, *or* b) the word used seems to change for no apparent reason in two similar sentences, *or* c) there is no preposition at all in French where there is one in the English sentence:

au Canada	to *or* in Canada
en France	to *or* in France
à la gare	to (or at) the station
au premier étage	on the first floor
à pied	on foot
en voiture	by car, in a car
en deux heures	within two hours
j'habite Miami	I live in Miami
je cherche un poste	I'm looking for a job
j'ai payé ces articles	I've paid for these articles
regardez cette facture	look at this bill
j'aime écouter la radio	I like listening to the radio

To/at/in   à   au   à la   à l'   aux
The basic word for to/at/in is **à** but it changes its spelling according to the word that follows it. The rule is:

à before any proper noun (but see **au** below)
changez à Nancy   change at Nancy

ce train va à Besançon?	is this train going to Besançon?
je voudrais parler à Monsieur Deferre	I'd like to speak to Mr. Deferre

au before any masculine singular noun beginning with a consonant, including the names of masculine countries

jusqu'au boulevard	up to the boulevard
au carrefour	at/to the intersection
nous voudrions parler au directeur	we'd like to speak to the manager
au Canada	to/in Canada

NB: in/to + name of *feminine* countries = **en**

en France, en Espagne	to/in France, to/in Spain

à la before any feminine noun beginning with a consonant

passez à la caisse	go to the cash register

à l' before any singular noun beginning with a vowel

quel est l'autobus qui va à l'auberge de jeunesse?	which bus goes to the youth hostel?
je dois aller à l'hôpital?	do I have to go to hospital?

aux before any plural noun

pour aller aux magasins, s'il vous plaît?	what's the way to the stores, please?
aux Etats-Unis	to/in the United States

Note also the following usages of **à, au, à la, à l', aux** which do not correspond with the way English expresses the same idea:

ma voiture est à deux kilomètres de cette cabine SOS	my car is two kilometers away from this emergency telephone
le menu à 28 francs	the 28 franc menu
un timbre à 1 franc 20	a 1 franc 20 stamp
des cigarettes à la menthe	menthol cigarettes
un baba au rhum	a rum baba
une glace à la fraise	a strawberry ice cream
une tranche de gâteau aux amandes	a slice of almond cake
un chausson aux pommes	an apple turnover
un sandwich au fromage	a cheese sandwich
du saucisson à l'ail	some garlic sausage

USAGES:

Saying or finding out where something is

nous habitons à quinze kilomètres de Houston	we live 15 kilometers from Houston
vous travaillez à Rouen?	do you work in Rouen?
vous tournez au deuxième carrefour	you turn at the second intersection
au premier étage	on/at the first floor

Asking the way on foot, or finding out if you can use public transportation

l'autobus va à la gare maritime?	is the bus going to the harbor?
pour aller à la piscine?	how do I get to the swimming pool?
l'autobus s'arrête à la plage?	does the bus stop at the beach?
vous allez au centre de la ville?	are you going to the center of town?

Stating where your or someone else's aches and pains are, using the phrase **avoir mal à . . .** (see p.40)

j'ai mal aux oreilles	my ears ache
j'ai mal au pied	my foot hurts
ma fille a mal à l'oreille	my daughter's ear aches
mon fils a mal aux dents	my son has a toothache

Saying to whom you wish to speak

je voudrais parler . . .	I'd like to speak . . .
au directeur	to the manager
à la secrétaire	to the secretary
à Mlle Bouvreuil	to Miss Bouvreuil

Frequently to state the type of product you require

douze timbres à 1 franc 80	twelve 1 franc 80 stamps
je prends la bouteille à 23 francs	I'll take the 23 franc bottle
vous n'avez pas de cerises à 15 francs le kilo?	you don't have any cherries at 15 francs a kilo?
une glace à la vanille	a vanilla ice cream

Of/from de du de la de l' des

These words can mean 'of' or 'from' and, as in the case of **à**, **au**, **à la**, **à l'** and **aux** above, the spelling is dependent on the word which follows it.
de before a proper noun (but see **du** below)

je vais vous téléphoner de Bruxelles	I'll phone you from Brussels

du before any masculine singular noun beginning with a consonant, including the names of masculine countries

potage du jour	soup of the day
il vient du Canada	he comes from Canada

de la before any feminine singular noun beginning with a consonant

à 200 mètres de la plage	200 meters from the beach

de l' before any singular noun beginning with a vowel

au bout de l'année	at the end of the year
le montant de l'assurance	the price of the insurance

des before any plural noun

une liste des hôtels de la région	a list of the region's hotels
un horaire des trains à . . .	a timetable of the trains to . . .
le représentant des Etats-Unis	the representative of the United States

Since there is no apostrophe **s** in French, as in 'John's book', 'the manager's office' you will have to think in terms of 'the book of John', 'the office of the manager' and translate the 'of' into French using the correct form of **de, du, de la, de l'** and **des**

la voiture de Philippe	Philip's car
le bureau du directeur	the manager's office
le sac de la réceptionniste	the receptionist's purse
le bureau de l'aubergiste	the innkeeper's office
toilettes des enfants	children's toilets

de, du, de la, de l' and **des** also occur with many prepositions (or phrases doing the job of prepositions) which give locations. Note these examples:

près de	near to (in the vicinity of)	**loin de**	far from
en face de	across the street from	**à côté de**	next to
à droite de	on the right of	**à gauche de**	on the left of
près de Metz	near Metz	**loin de la ville**	far from the town

en face du supermarché opposite the supermarket
à côté des w.c. publics next to the public washrooms
à droite du parking to the right of the parking lot
à gauche de la gare routière to the left of the bus station

NB: **devant** in front of, a preposition which contrary to expectation is *not* followed by **de, du, de la, de l'** or **des**
devant le cinéma in front of the theater
devant la gare in front of the station

USAGES: Saying or asking where someone or something is from

vous venez du Portugal?	do you come from Portugal?
ce vin vient de l'Allemagne?	does this wine come from Germany?

To translate 'of'

un horaire des autobus	a bus timetable

To express the idea of ownership

ce sont les gants de votre femme?	are these your wife's gloves?
c'est le tricot de mon fils	it's my son's sweater

Talking about and understanding locations

c'est près de la mairie?	is it near city hall?
c'est en face de la boîte de nuit	it's across the street from the night club
c'est à côté du Bureau de la Sécurité Sociale	it's next to the Social Security Office

Question words

TIY: p.110

USAGES:
- finding out information
- understanding questions which people ask you

EXPLANATION: Knowing how to ask questions and being able to understand the questions which people ask you will be an important part of your language needs abroad.

If you're mainly interested in speaking French, then the easiest way to ask a question is to speak in a questioning tone of voice and add one of the following question words (**pourquoi?** why? **avec qui?** with whom? **quand?** when? **comment?** what?/how?) at the end of your sentence. Here are some examples:

vous allez où?	where are you going?
vous allez avec qui?	who are you going with?
vous y allez pourquoi?	why are you going there?

vous allez faire quoi?	what are you going to do?
vous revenez quand?	when are you coming back?
l'autobus arrive à quelle heure?	at what time does the bus arrive?
le train part à quelle heure?	at what time does the train leave?
il y a un autobus tous les combien?	how often is there a bus?
vous avez combien de succursales?	how many branches do you have?
vous avez combien d'enfants?	how many children do you have?
vous avez passé le weekend comment?	how did you spend the weekend?
votre appartement est comment?	what's your apartment like? (how is your apartment?)
vous vous appelez comment?	what's your name? (how are you called?)
il faut que je m'adresse à qui?	who must I speak to?
vous parlez de quoi?	what are you talking about?
vous venez d'où?	where do you come from?
vous êtes né quand?	when were you born?
vous êtes né où?	where were you born?
vous apprenez le français depuis quand?	how long have you been learning French?
vous êtes marié?	are you married?
vous désirez?	what would you like?
vous avez fini?	have you finished?
ah bon?	really?
tiens?	really? you don't say?

There are other ways, apart from simply raising your voice, of asking questions. You will often hear the phrase **est-ce que . . .?**: take this as a cue which signals a question rather than consciously translating the phrase

est-ce que vous avez fini?	have you finished?
est-ce que vous êtes marié?	are you married?
où est-ce que vous avez passé le weekend?	where did you spend the weekend?
à quelle heure est-ce que vous êtes arrivé?	at what time did you arrive?

You will also hear a longer form **qui** (who) **est-ce qui . . .?**

qui est-ce qui a téléphoné?	who telephoned?
qui est-ce qui a laissé ce message?	who left this message?

Another cue which signals a question is **n'est-ce pas?** (don't I? don't you? doesn't he? etc – in all persons and all tenses)

je tourne à gauche, n'est-ce pas?	I turn left, don't I?
vous avez tout ce qu'il faut, n'est-ce pas?	you've got everything you need, haven't you?
il est tombé, n'est-ce pas?	he fell, didn't he?

In written French you will generally see the inverted question form, where the subject and the verb are switched around from the normal word order and the verb comes first:

aimez-vous le fromage?	do you like cheese?
quelle heure êtes-vous arrivé?	at what time did you arrive?
pourquoi a-t-il quitté la maison?	why did he leave the house?

Which/what a + noun = **quel** + noun in French

The spelling of **quel** changes according to the noun which follows it. This is the rule:

quel before a masculine singular noun
quelle before a feminine singular noun
quels before a masculine plural noun
quelles before a feminine plural noun

quel homme?/!	which man? *or* what a man!
quelle femme?/!	which woman? *or* what a woman!
quels hommes?/!	which men? *or* what men!
quelles femmes?/!	which women? *or* what women!

However, since none of the extra letters changes the pronunciation of **quel**, the above pattern is given for reference: don't worry about the spelling if you are only interested in speaking the language.

Examples:

quel dommage!	what a shame!
quelle surprise!	what a surprise!
il faut prendre quelle ligne pour aller à . . .?	which bus route (or subway line) do I take to get to . . .?
le train part de quel quai et de quelle voie?	what platform and what track does the train leave from?
le bus pour . . . part de quel arrêt?	which stop does the bus for . . . leave from?
c'est quel arrêt?	which stop is this?
il est quelle heure?	what time is it?
quelle est votre adresse?	what's your address?
vous avez quel âge?	how old are you? (what is your age?)

quelle est votre date de naissance?	what's your date of birth?
quel est le moins cher?	which is cheaper/the cheapest?
quels sont les moins chers?	which are cheaper/the cheapest?

How much?/how many? is **combien**, but if followed by a noun you must put the word **de** (or **d'** in front of a word beginning with a vowel) *after* **combien** and *before* the noun:

c'est combien?	how much is that?
vous en voulez combien?	how much (or how many) do you want?
tu veux combien de fromage?	how much cheese do you want?
tu as combien de frères?	how many brothers have you got?
vous avez combien d'enfants?	how many children have you got?
vous arriverez dans combien de jours?	you'll arrive in how many days? (from now)
vous y avez travaillé combien d'années?	how many years did you work there?
qu'est-ce que vous avez comme . . . + noun	what sort of . . ./what type of . . .?

This is a very useful phrase:

qu'est-ce que vous avez comme desserts?	what sort of desserts do you have?
qu'est-ce que vous avez comme parfums?	what sorts of flavors do you have?
qu'est-ce que vous avez comme voiture?	what sort of car do you have?

NB: **parfum** means both 'perfume' and 'flavor'.

USAGES:

The wide variety of examples given in the explanation section shows how difficult it is to make a list of circumstances in which you use question forms. You will need to use them in practically every situation you come across in the foreign country, but perhaps especially when shopping, eating and drinking out, using public transportation and talking with people whom you meet about their backgrounds.

Try it yourself

Don't let your memories of tests and examinations at school discourage you in this section. The idea behind it is to give you some practice using the language before you go to a French-speaking country. As far as possible you will only be asked to say things you might actually have to say in a real-life situation.

Each section generally begins with some sentences to learn by heart. One way of tackling these is to begin by reading through the French and English sentences several times, then cover the English sentences and see if you can remember the meaning of the French sentences. Finally, cover the French sentences and see if you can remember them, leaving the English uncovered as a cue. Recording the sentences on a cassette recorder is a good idea. You could record your answers to many of the other activities too.

The activities are designed to test how well you have understood and remembered the grammar points in the book, so don't attempt 'try it yourself' activities until you've studied the relevant part of the book in some detail. The idea is also to extend and elaborate on the examples in the book, so that you are actually making up 'new' language, not just copying words written down for you. For this reason you may find words in the tests which are not in the main section of the book. Some of these you will have to guess (which is exactly what you would have to do in real life), others will be supplied for you. If you're the sort of person who likes to check every detail, then access to a dictionary would be helpful. You should, in any case, carefully consider buying a dictionary and a phrasebook to go with your *Nice 'n Easy French Grammar* if you are eager to cope with all linguistic eventualities on your trip abroad!

Don't forget that answers to most of the activities can be found in the section beginning on p.112.

The present

FOR LEARNING:

je m'appelle . . .	I'm called . . . (my name is . . .)
mon mari parle un peu de français	my husband speaks a little French
on sort maintenant	we're going out now
vous êtes marié?	are you married?
je regarde seulement	I'm only looking
nous cherchons une station de taxi	we're looking for a taxi stand
j'aime l'ail	I like garlic

A In each case, match up two sentence halves so that they make sense.
Then translate each sentence into English.

1 Je prends ce médicament   **a** est fiévreux
2 Vous avez   **b** six fois par jour
3 Mon mari   **c** des enfants?
4 Je suis   **d** ce soir?
5 Vous partez   **e** célibataire

B Make up sentences along the lines of this example:

to learn	**(apprendre)**	French	for 5 years
	j'apprends	**le français**	**depuis cinq ans**
	I've been learning	French	for five years
to work	**(travailler)**	I.B.M.	for 6 months
to be	**(être)**	sick	for 2 days
to wait	**(attendre)**	taxi	for 15 minutes
to live	**(habiter)**	Détroit	for 2 years

C In the sentences below, the verb has been left out. Choose a verb from the list above the sentences which will fit into the blank so that the sentences make sense. You will need to give the correct spelling of the verb in the present tense. Try to translate your completed sentences into English.

venir to come   **conduire** to drive   **aller** to go
mettre to put   **boire** to drink

1 Vous............................ une Renault 18?
2 Nous............................ du thé au petit déjeuner
3 Je................................ ça sur la table?
4 Je................................ le 17 septembre
5 On .... au cinéma?

The imperfect

A In each case, match up two sentence halves so that they make sense. Then translate each sentence into English.

1 j'étais   **a** dans un petit village
2 les aires de service   **b** une veste rouge
   (=expressway service areas)
3 ma femme travaillait   **c** épuisé
4 il portait   **d** étaient très propres en Suisse
5 nous habitions   **e** au Canada comme professeur

B Imagine that someone has asked you **'qu'est-ce que vous faisiez au moment exact où ...?'** what were you doing at the precise moment when ...? Work out what you would say using each of the verbs below, giving an answer first starting with **je ...**, then an answer starting with **nous ...**

Example: **boire** to drink   **je buvais** I was drinking
                                   nous buvions we were drinking

faire { **mes**   to pack { my
          { **nos valises**   { our suitcases
ralentir to slow down

tourner   to turn
descendre   to go down(stairs)
monter   to go up(stairs)
arriver   to arrive
partir   to leave
lire   to read
prendre le petit déjeuner   to have breakfast

The perfect

FOR LEARNING:

nous sommes allés trois fois en Espagne	we've been to Spain three times
je suis arrivé cet après-midi	I arrived this afternoon
nous sommes venus de Cherbourg	we've come from Cherbourg
je suis né le quinze novembre mil neuf cent cinquante	I was born on November 15, 1950
nos enfants sont restés à la maison	our children have stayed at home
nous sommes partis hier matin	we left yesterday morning
vous êtes rentré comment?	how did you get home?
mon mari est tombé	my husband has fallen
je suis retourné chez le médecin	I went back to the doctor's office
vous avez fait une erreur	you've made a mistake
je n'ai pas pu vous joindre	I wasn't able to reach you (by phone)
je n'ai pas compris	I haven't understood
nous avons dormi très mal	we slept very badly
vous avez vu ce film?	have you seen this movie?

A The following sentences are supposed to be in the perfect tense, but as you can see something is missing. When you know what is missing, try to translate the complete sentence into English.

1 J ....dormi très mal
2 J ....allé en Allemagne l'année dernière
3 Nous....................restés à l'hôtel
4 J ....arrivé hier matin
5 Nous....................compris
6 J ....fait une erreur
7 J ....né en 1947

B These sentences also have something missing. From the list of verbs choose the one which will best fill each blank. Remember the verbs are in the infinitive form and you have to change each one into a past participle before it goes into the blank.

acheter to buy; **disparaître** to disappear (irreg.);
lire to read (irreg.); **perdre** to lose; **finir** to finish

1 Nous avons.......... , merci.
2 Mon fils a ....!
3 On a ....beaucoup de cadeaux (lots of presents).
4 Je n'ai pas.............ce roman (this novel).
5 J'ai ....ma montre (my watch).

C How would you say?
1 We went to Switzerland 2 My husband stayed home 3 Did you leave this morning? 4 We went back to the U.S.A. 5 Did you sleep well? 6 Did you understand? 7 I've seen this movie 8 What (**qu'est-ce que**) did you do? 9 Did you arrive safe and sound (**sain et sauf**)? 10 You stayed for how long (**combien de temps**)? 11 We bought a watch 12 I've finished, thanks 13 I read the newspaper (**le journal**) 14 I left yesterday morning.

Venir de + infinitive

A Memorize and write out the present tense of **venir**.

B Use this table to help you with the practice activities below.

Je Mon mari Ma femme Mon fils Ma fille Nous Mes amis Mes parents	viens vient venons viennent	de d'	manger arriver téléphoner partir

1 How would you say?
I just arrived. My wife has just left. My son just telephoned. My parents have just eaten.

2 Make up as many sentences as you can using the table above. Make sure you choose the right verb form from the second column for the subject, e.g. **je viens de manger**.

The pluperfect

A The following verbs in the infinitive form all appear in the pluperfect tense in the sentences below. Try to translate the sentences into English.

comprendre to understand **voir** to see
faire to do **se lever** to get up **recevoir** to receive
promettre to promise **s'attendre** to expect

1 Je ne m'étais pas attendu à cela (that)
2 Nous avions déjà fait cela
3 Mon mari s'était levé avant (before) moi
4 On avait déjà vu le film
5 Il n'avait pas reçu ma lettre
6 Je n'avais pas compris cela
7 On nous avait promis

The future

A Read these extracts from a letter you have received from a French hotel manager.

Quelles seront les dates probables de votre séjour? Vous arriverez en mi-semaine ou en fin de semaine? Est-ce que vous prendrez la demi-pension ou la pension complète? Vous viendrez en voiture? Un parking sera à votre disposition derrière l'hôtel. ... Les prix indiqués sont valables jusqu'au 15 juin. A partir de cette date-là le tarif sera plus élevé. ... Est-ce que vous aurez besoin d'une chaise haute pour votre bébé? Vos deux garçons partageront-ils une chambre?

If you wanted to translate this, you would have to understand the verbs in the future tense. As a practice activity make a list of every verb in the future tense and write down its infinitive form. Review your irregular future stems from the future column in the verb tables on p.124 before you start.

B Imagine you heard the following extracts on French radio:

France Inter – il est sept heures moins trois. Voici maintenant la météo avec Réné Chaboud ... Il a fait très beau sur toute la France hier mais les températures ont baissé au cours de la nuit et il fait très frais en ce moment sur la moitié nord. Dans le Midi il fait plus doux avec des bancs de brouillard matinaux qui se dissiperont sous peu. En début de journée le temps restera frais. Les averses seront fréquentes au nord. Demain le temps restera instable et se dégradera au cours de la journée ... Nous venons d'apprendre que la circulation est au ralenti sur le périphérique sud à cause des travaux. Faites attention – ne roulez pas trop vite.

Try to answer these questions about the broadcast, bearing in mind that it is mainly the identification of the future tense which is being practiced.

1 Are the temperatures going down at night or have they already gone down? **2** In the northern half (**moitié**) of France is it cool now or is it going to get cool? **3** In the South (**Midi**) are the banks of fog (**brouillard**) going to lift or have they already lifted? **4** Where will showers (**averses**) be frequent? **5** What will happen to the weather tomorrow in the course of the day (**au cours de la journée**)? **6** Is the traffic on the southern peripheral road going to slow down (**au ralenti**) or has it already slowed down because of road construction?

The conditional

FOR LEARNING

je voudrais une chambre à deux lits, s'il vous plaît	I'd like a room with twin beds, please
nous aimerions prendre le petit déjeuner dans notre chambre	we'd like to have breakfast in our room
je voudrais régler la facture, s'il vous plaît	I'd like to settle the bill, please
si je payais en dollars, ça couterait combien?	if I paid in dollars, how much would it cost?
s'il y avait un problème, la garantie serait valable aux Etats-Unis?	if there were a problem, would the guarantee be valid in the United States?

A Use this table to help you with the practice activities below.

Je		un citron pressé
Mon mari		un sandwich au fromage
Ma femme		une bière pression
Mon fils	voudrais	soixante francs de super
Ma fille	voudrait	habiter à la campagne
Mon collègue	voudrions	changer d'emploi
Ma collègue		prendre la retraite
Nous		acheter une nouvelle voiture

1 How would you say?
I would like a cheese sandwich. My (male) colleague would like a draft beer. My wife would like to change her job. We would like to live in the country. My husband would like to retire.

2 Make up as many sentences as you can using the above table. Make sure you choose a verb from the second column that fits the subject of the sentence, e.g. **ma fille voudrait changer d'emploi, nous voudrions acheter une nouvelle voiture**.

The conditional perfect

A Read this collection of newspaper headlines; then try to answer the questions below. Keep in mind that recognition of the conditional perfect is the main point of the activity.

'Attentat terroriste: des armes seraient de fabrication russe. ... Un D.C. 10 se serait écrasé au Luxembourg. ... Mme Thatcher s'est rendue au Japon. ... 47 ont trouvé la mort à la suite d'un accident ferroviare en Italie. ... Mouvement de grève dans les transports publics aurait été bien suivi. ... Explosion à Nancy – 13 victimes auraient été transportés d'urgence à l'hôpital. ... Fusillade à Paris – les agents ont tiré les premiers. ... Sommet Européen – des entretiens entre Kohl et Andreotti auraient déjà eu lieu. ...'

1 Were the terrorist arms definitely of Russian manufacture? 2 Is the D.C. 10 crash definite? 3 Has Mrs. Thatcher gone to Japan? 4 Are the reports of the 47 deaths in the Italian rail disaster definite? 5 Was the transportation strike definitely well supported? 6 Is the toll of 13 victims in the Nancy explosion only provisional? 7 Are the policemen in Paris reported to have fired or did they definitely fire first? 8 Have the talks at the European Summit already taken place or is this unconfirmed?

The imperative

FOR LEARNING

allons-y!	let's go!
ne quittez pas!	don't go! (don't hang up!)
vous me passez l'eau, s'il vous plaît?	will you please hand me the water?
on va manger maintenant?	shall we eat now?

A Read these real-life examples of instructions. If you wanted to find out the exact meanings, you would first have to make a list of the verbs in their infinitives forms, i.e. the spelling which they would have as entries in a dictionary. Identify all the verbs in the instructions and write down the list of infinitives, e.g. the first verb in the first instruction would appear as **décrocher** in the dictionary. Logically, you might write down **décrochre** as a possibility, but remember statistically **-er** verbs are the most common.

Décrochez le combiné. Introduisez une pièce de 50 centimes, 1F ou 5F. Attendez la tonalité. Composez le numéro.

Battez le jaune d'un œuf, ajoutez peu à peu la farine, le lait et un peu de sel. Remuez.

Gardez votre ticket.   Ouvrez ici.

Ralentissez.   Mettez votre ceinture.

B For oral practice try saying all the following commands or requests in three different ways, e.g. **mettre cela par écrit**   to put that in writing mettez cela par écrit s'il vous plaît! voulez-vous mettre cela par écrit? on va mettre cela par écrit?

manger quelque chose	signer les papiers
boire quelque chose	fixer les tarifs
partir maintenant	regarder les échantillons (look at
aller au cinéma	the samples)
prendre un dessert	
fixer un rendez-vous	

C The table will help you with further oral practice.

apporter (to bring)	des pommes à 6F le kilo	
donner (to give)	le poivre (pepper)	s'il
mettre (to put)	un biftek bien cuit (steak well-done)	vous
passer (to pass)	un blanc-cassis (white wine and blackcurrant apéritif)	plaît

How would you say?

1 Put (in my bag) some apples at 6F per kilo, please.

2 Bring me steak well-done, please.

Now make up as many sentences as you can, e.g. Vous m'apportez un blanc-cassis, s'il vous plaît; Voulez-vous m'apporter un blanc-cassis, s'il vous plaît?

The infinitive

FOR LEARNING

on va partir demain	we're going to leave tomorrow
on doit payer?	do you have to pay?
qu'est-ce qu'il faut faire?	what do you have to do?
je préfère régler en espèces	I prefer to pay in cash
je ne sais pas nager	I can't swim
ma femme vient de vous parler	my wife just spoke to you
nous voulons voir un dentiste	we wish to see a dentist
on peut entrer par ici?	can we enter this way?

A How well do you know these useful verbs that are often accompanied by infinitives? Try to translate them:

1 I like to ... 2 We hope to ... 3 My wife has to ...
4 I feel like ... 5 Can one ...? 6 Do you have to ...?
7 I'm sorry to ... 8 We've just ...

B These five verbs have been omitted from the sentences below. Can you match them up correctly and then translate the sentences you have completed?
(avons, savez, dois, faut, a)

1 Vous .... conduire?
2 Nous .... envie de boire quelque chose.
3 Qu'est-ce qu'il .... faire?
4 Je .... téléphoner en Angleterre.
5 On .... l'intention de fixer les prix.

C Each of these sentences has something omitted. Rewrite them, putting back what has been left out.

1 Nous l'intention repartir en Amérique.
2 Ma femme envie manger quelque chose.
3 Nous commençons avoir chaud.
4 Mon fils vient se marier.
5 Je voudrais en argent anglais.

D Translate these 'sentence openers', all of which would be followed by an infinitive.

1 We've finished ... 2 I've tried to ... 3 My daughter has decided to ... 4 We've begun to ...

E Unscramble these sentences, then translate each one:

1 j'vous téléphoner de essayé ai
2 avons à 48F menu nous prendre de décidé le
3 à commencé avez vous l'anglais apprendre collège au?

F Use the table for oral practice, making up as many correct sentences as possible.

J' Ma femme Mon mari On Nous	ai a avons	décidé essayé fini	de d'	aller au théâtre faire un petit tour (have a stroll) prendre le menu à 100F faire marcher la douche (get the shower to work) manger consulter l'annuaire (look in the directory) faire du jogging

E.g. J'ai décidé d'aller au théâtre; Mon mari a essayé de faire marcher la douche; On a fini de consulter l'horaire; Nous avons décidé de faire un petit tour.

Expressions with *faire* and *avoir*

A Make sure you know the present tense of **avoir**, especially the **je**, **il/elle/on** and **nous** forms, before you translate these sentences:

1 We're no longer hungry (we're full) 2 My son is frightened of dogs 3 I'm cold 4 You're right 5 My husband is 35 6 We need a dentist

B Make sure you know the present tense of **faire**, especially the **je**, **il/elle/on** and **nous** forms, then try translating these sentences:

1 We're camping here   **2** We'd like to go on a trip   **3** Do you offer reductions?   **4** Do you serve meals?

D Match up these sentence halves so that they make sense, then translate the completed sentences into English.

1 Nous avons	**a** une promenade
2 Nous allons faire	**b** besoin de verres
3 On a envie de	**c** 11 ans
4 Mon fils a	**d** faire une excursion demain

The simple past

A If you ever needed to understand sentences containing the simple past tense it would generally be the verbs themselves whose meanings you would be checking, as key items of information. Read these sentences and see if you can make a list of the verbs in the infinitive form (as they would appear in a dictionary). Review the *Simple Past* in the verb tables (p.125) first.

Un miracle se produisit. . . . Ce fut le bruit de pas qui m'éveilla. . . . Ils firent quelques préparatifs immédiats. . . . Il parla d'une voix rauque. . . . J'eus un frisson d'horreur. . . . Il but son café d'un trait. . . . Des scènes atroces se déroulèrent. . . . Les Brésiliens attaquèrent les premiers. . . . Keegan marqua pendant la seizième minute. . . . L'Equipe Renault continua à dominer les opérations. . . . Personne ne fut surpris. . . . L'explosion fit 22 victimes. . . . Les marines de la force d'interposition multinationale se retirèrent hier soir.

Negatives

FOR LEARNING

je ne vous ai pas compris	I haven't understood you
je n'ai pas pu ouvrir la porte de ma chambre	I wasn't able (didn't manage) to open my bedroom door
je n'aime pas l'ail	I don't like garlic
nous n'avons pas d'enfants	we have no children
nous n'avons plus d'essence	we ran out of gas
je n'ai qu'un billet de cinquante francs	I've only got a 50F note
vous n'avez pas de sandwiches?	don't you have any sandwiches?
vous n'avez rien à boire?	don't you have anything to drink?

A Each of these sentences has something missing. Rewrite each one, putting back what has been left out.

1 Je ne vous ai vu
2 J'aime pas fromage
3 Nous n'avons un enfant
4 Ma sœur n'a pas enfants
5 Vous n'avez de bière?

B Match each of the questions with a suitable reply in the right-hand column

1 Vous avez visité le Centre Pompidou à Paris?

2 C'est tout ce que vous avez pour bagages?

3 C'est pour une chambre?

4 Je peux vous offrir une cigarette?

5 Vous avez de la monnaie?

6 Vous voulez manger quelque chose?

7 Ce n'est qu'une sortie de secours par ici.

8 Il y a quelqu'un avec vous?

a Merci, je ne fume plus.

b Non, rien, merci.

c Non, jamais.

d Je m'excuse. Je n'ai pas vu le panneau.

e Non, personne.

f Oui, je n'ai qu'une valise.

g Oui, nous avons réservé d'avance.

h Je n'ai qu'un billet de 100F.

The definite article

FOR LEARNING

où sont les produits congelés?	where are the frozen foods?
c'est le mardi deux juin	it's Tuesday, June 2nd
pourriez vous vérifier l'huile?	could you check the oil?
je fréquente des cours du soir le lundi et le mercredi	I go to night school classes on Mondays and Wednesdays
c'est combien les cent grammes?	how much is it per 100 grams?
c'est combien la boîte?	how much is it per can (box)?
j'aime les petits pois	I like peas

A   Write out these nouns with the correct word for 'the' in front of them. You will need to get a dictionary.
pneu; boulangerie; tube; ail; orange; dame

  1   Why is it possible to write the correct word for 'the' for **ail** and **orange** without checking in a dictionary?

  2   Why could you write **la** in front of **dame** without checking in a dictionary?

B   Now write the plurals of all the words above (leaving out 'garlic', which doesn't really have a plural), putting the correct French word for 'the' in front.

C   Write out these dates in English:
le vendredi 23 décembre; le samedi 1er mai; le jeudi 30 avril; le lundi 7 août.

D   Write out these dates in French, following the pattern above:
Thursday, December 1; Monday, August 23; Saturday, April 7.

E   How would you say in French?
  1 We'll arrive (nous arriverons) on Friday, May 30 **2** Can you come on Fridays? **3** Can you come on Friday?

F   Use the table on the next page for oral practice.

C'est combien		le la les	paquet? boîte? bouteille? litre? livre? kilo? deux cents grammes?

How would you say?
1 How much is it per box?   2 How much is it per liter?   3 How much is it per 200 grams?
Make up as many sentences as you can to ask the price per unit.

Imagine you have looked up these words in a dictionary:

ail (m) garlic, **saucisson** (m) sausage, **escargot** (m) snail, **cuisse de grenouille** (f) frog's leg, **gras** (m) fat (on meat), **chocolat à croquer** (m) plain chocolate, **frite** (f) French fry, **sport** (m) sport, **télévision** (f) television, **natation** swimming.

Say whether you like or dislike each of the above, e.g.
ah oui, j'aime le saucisson   oh yes, I like sausage
ah non, je n'aime pas les cuisses   oh no, I don't like frog's legs
   de grenouille

Be careful not to leave out the words for 'the' in French!

The indefinite article

FOR LEARNING

on voudrait louer une voiture	we'd like to rent a car
vous avez un horaire?	do you have a timetable?
vous vendez des journaux américains?	do you sell any American newspapers?
moi, je prends une côtelette de porc avec des pommes vapeur	I'll have a pork chop with boiled potatoes
vous avez un plan du quartier?	do you have a map of the area?
nous cherchons une vendeuse	we're looking for a sales lady

A Imagine you have looked up these words in a dictionary:

collant (m) (pair of) pantyhose; **timbre** (m) (postage) stamp; **portion** (f) portion; **glace** (f) ice cream; **salade de fruits** (f) fruit salad.

1 How would you say?

a pair of pantyhose   an ice cream   a fruit salad
some/any stamps   some/any ice creams

2 What has been left out in these sentences?
Vous avez timbres?   Moi, je voudrais glace
Vous avez collants?

B Use the snack and drink list on the next page for oral practice by asking for something to eat and drink for yourself. Your order could start with either **moi, je prends ...** (I'll have ...) or **je voudrais ...** (I would like ...). Remember that the next word will be either **un**, **une** or **des** ....

Sandwiches variés: au fromage
                       au jambon
                       au saucisson

Omelettes: nature (plain)
                aux champignons (mushrooms)

Glaces (choix de parfums):   à la fraise (strawberry)
                                   à la vanille
                                   au chocolat

                 *   *   *

Vin rouge
    blanc
    rose

Eau minérale
Limonade

Bière: en bouteille
       pression

Whisky
Pastis
Cognac

Translate into French:

1 I'll have French fries and peas   **2** Do you have any children?   **3** I have friends in Paris   **4** I'm a salesman/saleswoman   **5** My brother's a rep (**représentant**)   **6** My father's a policeman (**agent de police**).

The partitive

FOR LEARNING

vous avez de la place?	do you have any room?
où puis je trouver de l'huile?	where can I find some oil?
du pâté pour quatre personnes, s'il vous plaît	some pâté for four people, please
il n'y a pas de cintres dans l'armoire	there are no coat hangers in the wardrobe
je n'ai pas de monnaie	I don't have any change

A If you had looked up these words in the dictionary

scotch (m) cellophane tape; **moutarde** (f) mustard; **glace** (f) ice cream; **sparadrap** (m) adhesive gauze; **confiture** (f) jam; **eau** (f) water

how would you say?

some water; some jam; some mustard; some cellophane tape; some adhesive gauze; some ice cream; some ice creams.

B Translate into English:

des pains; du pain; des aspirines; de l'aspirine; de la glace; des glaces

C How would you say?

1 I don't have any tape **2** We don't have any mustard **3** Don't you have any jam? **4** There's no water on the table.

D Use the table on the next page for oral practice. Don't forget the word you choose from the second column depends on what you choose from the third column, e.g.

Il y a du porc? is there any pork? (**porc** is masculine)

Où puis je trouver de la salade? Where can I find some lettuce? (**salade** is feminine)

Vous avez de l'eau? Do you have any water? (**eau** begins with a vowel)

Je voudrais des artichauts I'd like some artichokes (**artichauts** is plural)

			saucisson (m)	(sausage)
			porc (m)	
			boeuf (m)	(beef)
			fromage (m)	
Je voudrais	du		poulet (m)	
Vous avez	de la		riz (m)	(rice)
Il y a	de l'		artichaut (m)	
Où puis-je trouver	des		crème (f)	
			huile (f)	
			eau (f)	
			poire (f)	(pear)
			salade (f)	

Unscramble these sentences (of complaint!) and translate them into English:

1 de pas n'y il pain a
2 il ampoule w.c. le n'y dans pas a d'
3 baignoire (bath) bonde il pas a n'y de la dans

In each of these sentences something has been left out. Rewrite them putting back what is missing; then translate into English.

1 Nous aimerions bien prendre la glace
2 Vous n'avez pas frites?
3 Je voudrais l'eau s'il vous plaît
4 Vous avez riz?
5 Il n'y a pas ampoule dans la lampe de chevet (bedside)
6 Il n'y a pas papier hygiénique dans les toilettes

Expressions of quantity

FOR LEARNING

cinquante litres d'essence	50 liters of gasoline
un kilo de bananes	1 kilo of bananas
quatre tranches de jambon	four slices of ham
une livre de beurre	1 lb. of butter
un peu de crème	a little cream
trop de sel	too much salt

A How would you say?
6 slices; 2 pairs; 3 liters; 4 portions; 2½ kilos; 2 packages; 3 boxes; 6 cups; 2 jars; ½ bottle

B Match the quantities in the lefthand column with a product in the righthand column, choosing the correct word for 'of' from the middle column. Then translate into English the phrases you have assembled.

trois tranches				miel (honey)
une bouteille				oranges
un demi-kilo		de		gâteau
une boîte		d'		allumettes (matches)
un tube				aspirines
un pot				huile d'olive

C Something is missing from each of these phrases. Rewrite them, putting back what has been left out.
un verre eau minérale; une tranche quiche lorraine; deux tasses thé au lait

D Translate one language into the other:
1 Vous avez assez de sauce? **2** Un peu de poivre? **3** Trop de frites? **4** A little sauce **5** Enough French fries? **6** Too much pepper?

Pronouns

Would you use **tu** or **vous** in each of the following cases?

1 when addressing a customs officer 2 when addressing a little boy 3 when addressing an old friend 4 when addressing a post office clerk.

How many *different* ways in English could this French phrase be translated:

on accepte la carte bleue (Visa Card) **ici**

Look very closely at the pronouns in each of these sentences and try to answer the questions in English.

1 Je vous verrai demain soir. — Whom is the person going to see tomorrow evening?

2 Je vous les enverrai demain. — What is this person going to send you tomorrow?

3 Je la connais très bien. — Whom does this person know well?

4 Je l'ai vu hier. — Whom did this person see yesterday?

5 Les Metro anglaises? Elles ont bonne presse. — Who or what gets a good write-up?

6 Rocky Trois? Je l'ai vu hier soir avec Sylvie. — Did the person speaking want to tell you mainly about seeing Sylvie last night?

7 Les toilettes? Elles sont en face de l'Hôtel de Ville. — Who are the females across the street from City Hall?

8 Il m'a donné un coup de téléphone. — Did the person speaking call someone up or did someone call the person up?

9 On nous a écrit. — Did someone write to us or did we write to someone?

10 Je dois leur montrer mon passeport? — What's your question about your passport?

11 Je dois lui parler. — To whom do you have to speak?

12 Je ne vous comprends pas. — Are you saying you don't understand the other person or asking the other person if they understand you?

D Using the emphatic pronouns, how would you say?
for me; for you; without her; with him; it belongs to them; it's my turn;
at our place; at your place.

E Use the table for oral practice.

Maintenant (now)		c'est à	moi
Si on allait (supposing we went)		chez	toi
Je vais		avec	lui
Ne partez pas		pour	elle
C'est un cadeau (it's a present)		sans	nous
C'est un pourboire (it's a tip)			vous
			eux
			elles

Make up as many logical sentences as you can, e.g.

Maintenant c'est à moi; Si on allait chez vous? Je vais avec lui; Ne
partez pas sans eux; C'est un cadeau pour elle; C'est un pourboire
pour vous;

Adjectives

FOR LEARNING

nous avons un petit appartement	we have a small apartment
une grande bière, s'il vous plaît	a large beer, please
j'ai laissé un sac en cuir noir?	did I leave a black leather purse?
une Ford jaune à hayon arrière	a yellow Ford with a hatchback
vous avez quelque chose en daim?	do you have something in suede?

A Unscramble these phrases, then translate each one into English:

1 chemise blanche une
2 un rouge pullover
3 Buick une noire
4 café petit un
5 un repas long
6 bon un restaurant
7 une raison (reason) bonne

B In addition to the vocabulary you have learned in this section, learn these additional words and phrases:

grand tall; **roux** red (of hair); **blond** blond; **aux yeux . . .** with . . . eyes; **bleu** blue

Now, translate the following descriptions into French (use the sentences below as examples):

c'est un petit garçon aux cheveux he's a little boy with blond hair
blonds et aux yeux bruns and brown eyes
c'est une grande fille aux cheveux she's a tall girl with black hair and
noirs et aux yeux verts green eyes

1 He's a tall boy with red hair and brown eyes
2 He's a little boy with black hair and green eyes
3 She's a tall girl with brown hair and brown eyes
4 She's a little girl with blond hair and blue eyes

C Using the vocabulary you have learned with these additional words
jupe (f) skirt; **blouson** (m) windbreaker; **robe** (f) dress
how would you say?

1 She's wearing (**elle porte**) a green dress
2 He's wearing (**il porte**) a black jacket
3 She's wearing a white skirt
4 He's wearing a blue windbreaker

D Use the three boxes of words to make up sentences for oral practice.

mon portefeuille	gris	en cuir
mon pullover	bleu	en pvc
mon sac	vert	en plastique
mon imper	blanc	en daim
mon bracelet à breloques	rouge	en toile
(my charm bracelet)	brun	en coton
mon collier (my necklace)	noir	en argent (in silver)
mes boucles d'oreille	petit	en or (in gold)
(my earrings)	grand	

Either practice saying what has been stolen, e.g.
on m'a volé mon petit portefeuille   someone has stolen my little brown
  en cuir brun   leather wallet
Or practice saying what you have lost, e.g.
j'ai perdu mon imper en rouge   I've lost my red raincoat

E How would you say?
It was (c'était) . . . a good restaurant   a good hotel   a long trip
an interesting book   a bad movie   an interesting play.

F Use the table to help you talk about how you found things, places or
experiences.

Nous avons trouvé (we found)	ce café
	cette station
	  (this resort)
	ce voyage
	ce film
	ce livre
	cette pièce
	cette ville
	  (this town)
	ce village
	ce camping
	ce magasin
	  (this shop)
	ce supermarché
	  (this supermarket)
	cette région
	cet hôtel
	ce restaurant
		cher (expensive)
		chère (expensive)
		bon marché (cheap)
		long(ue)
		intéressant(e)
		ennuyeux (boring)
		ennuyeuse (boring)
		bruyant(e)
		commercialisé(e)
		affairé(e) (busy)
		pittoresque
		charmant(e)
		  (charming)

The alternate spellings of the adjectives in column 3 are the feminine
endings which you will need if you are talking about something
feminine in column 2. All the nouns with the word **cette** (this) in front
of them are feminine and all those with **ce** or **cet** (this) are masculine.
Here are a couple of examples:

Nous avons trouvé ce film ennuyeux; Nous avons trouvé cette pièce
ennuyeuse

Make up as many sentences as you can.

Possessives

FOR LEARNING

ce sont nos places	these are our seats
c'est ma voiture	it's my car
c'est votre mari?	is this your husband?
ma clef, s'il vous plaît	my key, please
notre chambre est à quel étage?	our room is on what floor?
il faut montrer nos billets?	do we have to show our tickets?
ce sont vos lunettes de soleil?	are these your sunglasses?

A If you had found these words in a dictionary
addition (f)   bill (in restaurant); **facture** (f)   bill (in hotel or garage);
bic (m)   ballpoint; **collègue** (m and f)   colleague; **place** (f)   seat;
secrétaire (m and f)   secretary
how would you say?
my ballpoint; our hotel bill; your colleagues; my secretary; our seats.

What would be the English translation of:
nos collègues; votre facture; leurs places; ses collègues; ton bic.

B Match up the sentence halves in the two columns, then translate the
completed sentences.

1	On m'a volé	**a**	votre fille?
2	Nous avons perdu	**b**	mon dentier
3	J'ai perdu	**c**	ses verres de contact
4	Cette dame a cassé	**d**	notre clef
5	C'est une photo de	**e**	montrer nos passeports?
6	Nous sommes obligés de	**f**	mon permis de conduire

Demonstratives

FOR LEARNING

vous acceptez cette carte de crédit?	do you accept this credit card?
je voudrais des piles comme ça	I'd like some batteries like that
je n'aime pas cette chambre	I don't like this room
cette table-ci?	this table?
vous pourrez me contacter à cette adresse-ci	you will be able to contact me at this address

A If you had found these words in the dictionary
bic (m) ballpoint; **pneu** (m) tire; **chaussure** (f) shoe; **poire** (f) pear;
comprimé (m) tablet; **restaurant** (m) restaurant; **hôtel** (m) hotel;
tasse (f) cup; **voiture** (f) car
how would you say?
this car; that restaurant; this cup; that car; this ballpoint;
those tablets; these tires; those shoes; these pears.

B How would you say in French?
1 I prefer those pears. **2** I like this restaurant. **3** I need that. **4** A
ballpoint like that.

Comparative and superlative

FOR LEARNING

vous avez quelque chose de moins cher?	do you have something less expensive?
on prend le plus doux	we'll take the sweetest (wine)
quel est le plus cher?	which is the most expensive?
pour la station de service la plus proche, s'il vous plaît?	the way to the nearest service station, please?

A If you had found these adjectives in a dictionary
affairé busy; **charmant** charming; **commercialisé** commercialized; **difficile** difficult; **ennuyeux** boring; **facile** easy; **pratique** handy
how would you say?
It is (c'est) ....
It was (c'était) ....
It would be (ce serait) ....
We found it (nous l'avons trouvé) ....
more boring; less boring; more commercialized; less busy; the most charming; the most difficult; the least handy; easier.

B Using these words
clair light (in color); **fort** strong; **large** wide; **long** long; **moderne** modern; **nouveau** new; **pétillant** sparkling; **sombre** dark; **typique** typical
how would you say?
Do you have something ... stronger?; less wide?; longer?; more modern?; newer?; less sparkling?; darker?; more typical?; less light?

C Imagine you are offered a choice of wines, in the first case a dry and a less dry (sec), secondly a sparkling and less sparkling (pétillant), finally a sweet and a less sweet (doux). Practice saying in each case 'we'll have the more ...... one', then 'we'll have the less ...... one'. Also practice asking 'which is the more ......?', 'which is the less ......?'

D Use the table for oral practice. Remember your choice of the word for 'the' in column 3 depends on the word you chose in column 2.

Où est (Where is) Où sont (Where are)	le supermarché le bureau de poste le restaurant la pharmacie la station de service les toilettes les magasins	le la les	plus proche(s)

Adverbs

FOR LEARNING

c'est absolument scandaleux	it's absolutely scandalous
c'est tout à fait inacceptable	it's absolutely unacceptable
c'est peu raisonnable	it's hardly reasonable (not very reasonable at all)
le vol s'est très bien passé	the flight went very well
la traversée s'est passée très rapidement	the crossing went very quickly
c'est très dangereux	it's very dangerous

A Use this table for oral practice and to help you answer the questions below.

C'est		assez		aigre (sour)
		très		amer (bitter)
		peu		sucré (sweet)
		trop (too)		corsé (strong, spicy)

How would you say?
It's . . . very sweet; too sour; not very spicy at all; fairly bitter; too sweet.

The word 'every'

FOR LEARNING

ce train circule tous les jours?	does this train run every day?
vous êtes ouvert tout l'hiver?	are you open all winter?
il y a un autobus tous les combien?	how often is there a bus?
nous y allons tous les trois mois	we go there every three months
vous serez fermé toute la semaine?	will you be closed all week?

A How would you say in English?
tous les samedis; toute la saison; toute l'année; tous les deux ans; toutes les trente minutes; tous les quarts d'heure.

B Unscramble these sentences, then translate each sentence into English:

1 métro a un y combien les tous il?
2 toutes minutes la revient dix les douleur
3 femme ma ce prend médicament les heures six toutes

Prepositions

FOR LEARNING

1 To / at / in

il faut changer à Besançon?	do you have to change at Besançon?
nous allons à Kassel en Allemagne	we're going to Kassel in Germany
je voudrais parler à Monsieur Michel	I'd like to speak to Mr. Michel
quel est l'autobus qui va à la gare?	which bus goes to the station?
le menu à quarante francs, s'il vous plaît	the 40-franc meal, please
une glace à la vanille, s'il vous plaît	a vanilla ice cream, please
c'est au deuxième étage?	is it on the second floor?
j'ai mal au doigt	my finger hurts
Manchester est à trois cents kilomètres de Londres	Manchester is 300 kilometers from London

A Choose a word from the list below to complete the sentences. Translate the completed sentences.
plage (f); parking (m); poubelles (f. pl); aéroport (m); Metz (name of French town).

1 Quel est l'autobus qui va à l'............?
2 Je dois aller aux ....
3 Vous vous arrêtez à la ....?
4 Pour aller à ...., s'il vous plaît?
5 Vous allez au ....?

B Something has been left out of each of these sentences. Rewrite them putting back what has been left out, then translate the completed sentences into English.
dos (m) back; **tête** (f) head.

1 Ma femme a mal l'oreille
2 Mon fils a mal oreilles
3 J'ai mal dents
4 Mon mari a mal la tête
5 Ma fille a mal dos

C How would you say in French?
1 Look at my car! **2** Listen to my husband! **3** I'm looking for a parking lot! **4** I'm paying (**c'est moi qui paie**) for the beer **5** to Spain/in Spain **6** to Strasburg/in Strasburg **7** on the third floor **8** by bus (same pattern as 'by car') **9** a ham sandwich **10** the five franc package **11** five two franc stamps

FOR LEARNING

2 Of / from

je vous téléphonerai de Luton	I'll phone you from Luton
je vous parle de la part d'un collègue	I'm speaking to you on behalf of a colleague
notre hôtel est à cinq cents metres du lac	our hotel is 500 meters from the lake
vous avez un horaire des vols à Philadelphie?	do you have a timetable of flights to Philadelphia?
je vous reverrai au début de l'année	I'll see you again at the beginning of the year
vous venez de quel coin de la France?	what corner (part) of France do you come from?
c'est en face du supermarché?	is it across the street from the supermarket?

A Match the phrase or sentence halves so they make sense, then translate the completed phrases or sentences.

1 plat (dish)   a Portugal
2 affaire (bargain)   b États-Unis
3 Ce monsieur vient des   c du jour
4 Je vous téléphonerai de   d de l'année
5 Ma femme vient du   e Paris

B Match the words in column 1 with the words in column 2, so they make sense.

The 'owners'	'Who or what is owned'
aubergiste (m/f) manager (of youth hostel)	l'appartement (apartment)
enfants (m/f pl) children	le bureau (office)
gérant (m) manager	le fils (son)
proprietaire (m/f) owner	la fille (daughter)
M. Kuhn (someone's name)	la piscine (swimming pool)
	la voiture (car)

e.g.
C'est le bureau de l'aubergiste?   Is it the manager's office?
C'est l'appartement de M. Kuhn?   Is it M. Kuhn's apartment?
C'est la fille du gérant?   Is it the manager's daughter?

C Match up the two halves of phrases from the two columns, then translate the completed phrases.

1 près de   a gare maritime (harbor)
2 loin du   b toilettes
3 à côté de la   c l'église (church)
4 en face des   d supermarché
5 à droite de   e Biarritz
6 à gauche de l'   f centre

D How would you say?
1 Is it near the supermarket? 2 Is it far from the airport? (aéroport (m)) 3 Is it near Lille? 4 Is it across the street from the parking lot? 5 Is it to the left of the rest rooms? 6 Is it in front of the bus station? (gare d'autobus (f))

Question words

(NB: practically all the examples in this section are useful enough to learn by heart. The examples below in the *For learning* section can only be a limited selection of the wide range of question forms used in everyday speech.)

FOR LEARNING

vous habitez où?	where do you live?
vous partez quand?	when are you leaving?
vous avez passé les vacances comment?	how did you spend your vacation?
c'est pour quoi?	what is it for?
ça coûte combien?	how much does that cost?
qui est à l'appareil?	who's speaking? (on the telephone)
est-ce que vous parlez anglais?	do you speak English?

A Match the sentence halves in the two columns below, then translate the completed sentences:

1 Vous acceptez   a de frères?
2 Votre maison   b à l'ordre de qui?
3 Vous êtes en vacances   c avec ma carte bleue (Visa Card)?
4 Vous avez combien   d n'est-ce pas?
5 Il faut faire le chèque   e tous les combien?
6 Est-ce que je peux régler (settle) f depuis quand?
7 Le service est compris   g est comment?
8 Il y a un autobus   h l'argent américain?

B Which questions would elicit these answers?
1 Je m'appelle Christiane Rozès 2 J'habite Morlaix en Bretagne 3 J'ai deux sœurs 4 C'est un grand appartement moderne avec trois chambres 5 Il y a un métro toutes les trois minutes 6 Oui, nous acceptons les dollars 7 Oui, toutes les taxes sont comprises 8 Il faut faire le chèque à l'ordre de 'Presto Cafétéria'

C Unscramble these sentences, then translate:

1 arrêt l'autobus Jarville pour quel de part?
2 part Thionville train le pour quel de quai?
3 pour prendre faut il à aller Châtelet ligne quelle?

D Could you reply in French to these official questions?
1 Quelle est votre adresse? 2 Quel est votre lieu (place) de naissance? 3 Quelle est votre date de naissance? 4 Vous avez quel âge?

E Using the model 'Qu'est-ce que vous avez comme parfums?' (What sort of ice cream flavors/perfumes have you got?), how would you say?

What sort of . . . hors d'oeuvres; sandwiches; cheeses; beers; wines; apartment; house; car; French newspapers (journaux français) do you have?

Answers to 'Try it yourself'

The present

A **1b** I take this medicine 6 times per day **2c** Do you have any children? **3a** My husband has a fever **4e** I'm a bachelor **5d** Are you leaving this evening?

B Je travaille pour I.B.M. depuis six mois; Je suis malade depuis deux jours; J'attends un taxi depuis quinze minutes; J'habite Détroit depuis deux ans.

C **1** conduisez Do you drive a Renault 18? **2** buvons We drink tea at breakfast **3** mets Do I put that on the table? **4** viens I'm coming on the 17th of September **5** va Are we going to the movies?

The imperfect

A **1c** I was exhausted **2d** The expressway service areas were very clean in Switzerland **3e** My wife used to work as a teacher in Canada **4b** He was wearing a red jacket **5a** We used to live in a small town.

B (the **je** form is given first) faisais mes .../faisions nos ...; ralentissais/ralentissions; tournais/tournions; descendais/descendions; montais/montions; j'arrivais/arrivions; partais/partions; lisais/lisions; prenais/prenions.

The perfect

A 1 J'ai ... I slept very badly 2 Je suis ... I went to Germany last year 3 sommes We stayed at the hotel 4 Je suis ... I arrived yesterday morning 5 avons We understood 6 J'ai ... I made a mistake 7 Je suis ... I was born in 1947.

B 1 fini 2 disparu 3 acheté 4 lu 5 perdu.

C 1 Nous sommes allés en Suisse 2 Mon mari est resté à la maison 3 Vous êtes parti ce matin? 4 Nous sommes retournés aux Etats-Unis 5 Vous avez (tu as ...) bien dormi? 6 Vous avez (tu as ...) compris? 7 J'ai vu ce film 8 Qu'est-ce que vous avez (tu as ...) fait? 9 Vous êtes (tu es ...) arrivé sain et sauf? 10 Vous êtes (tu es ...) resté combien de temps? 11 Nous avons acheté une montre 12 J'ai fini, merci 13 J'ai lu le journal 14 Je suis parti hier matin.

Venir de + infinitive

A je viens   tu viens   il/elle vient   nous venons   vous venez   ils/elles viennent.

B 1 Je viens d'arriver   Ma femme vient de partir   Mon fils vient de téléphoner   Mes parents viennent de manger.

2 Here are just some examples: Mon mari vient d'arriver   Ma femme vient de partir   Mon fils vient de téléphoner   Ma fille vient de manger   Nous venons de partir   Mes amis viennent d'arriver   Mes parents viennent de téléphoner.

The pluperfect

A **1** I hadn't expected that **2** We'd already done that **3** My husband had gotten up before me **4** We'd already seen the movie **5** He hadn't received my letter **6** I hadn't understood that **7** They'd promised us/we had been promised.

The future

A Seront – être; arriverez – arriver; prendrez – prendre; viendrez – venir; sera – être; sera – être; aurez – avoir; partageront – partager

B **1** already gone down **2** cool now **3** going to lift **4** in the North **5** it will get worse **6** already slowed down.

The conditional

A **1** Je voudrais un sandwich au fromage   Mon collègue voudrait une bière pression   Ma femme voudrait changer d'emploi   Nous voudrions habiter à la campagne   Mon mari voudrait prendre la retraite.

The conditional perfect

A **1** no **2** no **3** yes **4** yes **5** no **6** yes **7** definitely **8** unconfirmed.

The imperative

A décrocher . . . introduire . . . attendre . . . composer
battre . . . ajouter . . . remuer
garder
ouvrir
ralentir
mettre

B (first-type answers only)
mangez . . . buvez . . . partez . . . allez . . . prenez . . . fixez . . .
signez . . . fixez . . . regardez

C Vous me mettez des pommes à six francs le kilo, s'il vous plaît
Vous m'apportez un bifteck bien cuit, s'il vous plaît

The infinitive

A 1 J'aime 2 Nous espérons 3 Ma femme doit 4 J'ai envie de 5 On peut 6 On doit 7 Je m'excuse de 8 Nous venons de.

B 1 savez Can you drive? 2 avons We feel like drinking something 3 faut What do you have to do? 4 dois I must telephone England 5 We intend to fix the prices.

C 1 Nous *avons* l'intention *de* repartir en Amérique 2 Ma femme *a* envie *de* manger quelque chose 3 Nous commençons *à* avoir chaud 4 Mon fils vient *de* se marier 5 Je voudrais *régler* en argent anglais.

D 1 Nous avons fini de 2 J'ai essayé de 3 Ma fille a décidé de 4 Nous avons commencé à.

E 1 J'ai essayé de vous téléphoner – I tried to telephone you 2 Nous avons décidé de prendre le menu à 48F – We've decided to have the 48F meal 3 Vous avez commencé à apprendre l'anglais au collège? – Did you begin to learn English at school?

Expressions with *faire* and *avoir*

A 1 Nous n'avons plus faim 2 Mon fils a peur des chiens 3 J'ai froid 4 Vous avez (tu as . . .) raison 5 Mon mari a trente-cinq ans 6 Nous avons besoin d'un dentiste.

B 1 Nous faisons du camping ici 2 Nous voudrions faire une excursion 3 Vous faites une remise? 4 Vous faites restaurant?

C 1b We need (drinking) glasses 2a We're going to have a walk 3d We feel like going on a trip tomorrow 4c My son is 11 years old.

The simple past

A se produire être éveiller faire parler avoir boire se dérouler attaquer marquer continuer être faire se retirer.

Negatives

A 1 Je ne vous ai *pas* vu 2 Je *n*'aime pas *le* fromage 3 Nous n'avons *qu*'un enfant 4 Ma sœur n'a pas *d*'enfants 5 Vous n'avez *pas* de bière?

B 1c; 2f, 3g; 4a; 5h; 6b; 7d; 8e.

The definite article

A le pneu; la boulangerie; le tube; l'ail; l'orange; la dame.

1 because both words start with a vowel 2 because you knew that the noun referred to someone female.

B les pneus; les boulangeries; les tubes; les oranges; les dames.

C Friday, December 23; Saturday, May 1; Thursday, April 30; Monday, August 7.

D le jeudi 1er décembre; le lundi 23 août; le samedi 7 avril.

E 1 Nous arriverons le vendredi 30 mai . . . 2 Vous pouvez venir le vendredi? . . . 3 Vous pouvez venir vendredi?

F 1 C'est combien la boîte? 2 C'est combien le litre? 3 C'est combien les deux cents grammes?

G J'aime (or Je n'aime pas) . . . l'ail le saucisson les escargots les cuisses de grenouille le gras le chocolat à croquer les frites le sport la télévision la natation.

The indefinite article

A 1 un collant une glace une salade de fruits des timbres des glaces. 2 Vous avez *des* timbres? Moi, je voudrais *une* glace Vous avez *des* collants?

B . . . un sandwich une omelette une glace un vin une eau minérale une limonade une bière un whisky un pastis un cognac.

C 1 Moi je prends des frites et des petits pois 2 Vous avez des enfants? 3 J'ai des amis à Paris 4 Je suis vendeur (m)/vendeuse (f) 5 Mon frère est représentant 6 Mon père est agent de police.

The partitive

A   de l'eau; de la confiture; de la moutarde; du scotch; du sparadrap; de la glace; des glaces.

B   some loaves; some bread; some aspirins; some aspirin; some ice cream; some ice creams.

C   1 Je n'ai pas de scotch 2 Nous n'avons pas de moutarde 3 Vous n'avez pas de confiture? 4 Il n'y a pas d'eau sur la table.

D   du saucisson du porc du bœuf du fromage du poulet du riz des artichauts de la crème de l'huile de l'eau des poires de la salade.

E   1 Il n'y a pas de pain – There's no bread 2 Il n'y a pas d'ampoule dans le w.c. – There's no bulb in the toilet 3 Il n'y a pas de bonde dans la baignoire – There's no plug in the bath.

F   1 Nous aimerions bien prendre *de* la glace – We'd very much like some ice-cream 2 Vous n'avez pas *de* frites? – Don't you have any French fries? 3 Je voudrais *de* l'eau s'il vous plaît – I'd like some water, please 4 Vous avez *du* riz? – Do you have any rice? 5 Il n'y a pas *d'*ampoule dans la lampe de chevet – There's no bulb in the beside lamp 6 Il n'y a pas *de* papier hygiénique dans les toilettes – There's no toilet paper in the toilets.

Expressions of quantity

A   six tranches; deux paires; trois litres; quatre portions; deux kilos et demi; deux paquets; trois boîtes; six tasses; deux pots; une demi-bouteille.

B   trois tranches de gâteau – three slices of cake; une bouteille d'huile d'olive – a bottle of olive oil; un demi-kilo d'oranges – a ½ kilo of oranges; une boîte d'allumettes – a box of matches; un tube d'aspirines – a tube of aspirins; un pot de miel – a pot of honey.

C un verre *d'*eau minérale   une tranche *de* quiche lorraine   deux tasses *de* thé au lait.

D 1 Do you have enough sauce? 2 A little pepper? 3 Too many chips? 4 Un peu de sauce 5 Assez de frites? 6 Trop de poivre?

Pronouns

A 1 vous 2 tu 3 tu 4 vous.

B We accept ... they accept ... people accept ... The Visa Card is accepted here.

C 1 you 2 them 3 her 4 him or her 5 English Metros 6 No: the person speaking is saying he saw *it* last night, it being Rocky 3 7 the only 'females' is the female noun toilets! 8 someone gave the person a ring 9 someone wrote to us 10 do you have to show it to them? 11 to him or her 12 saying you don't understand the other person to whom you're talking.

D pour moi; pour vous (toi); sans elle; avec lui; c'est à eux (elles); c'est à moi; chez nous; chez vous (toi).

Adjectives

A 1 une chemise blanche – a white shirt 2 un pullover rouge – a red sweater 3 une Buick noire – a black Buick 4 un petit café – a small coffee (or café) 5 un long repas – a long meal 6 un bon restaurant – a good restaurant 7 une bonne raison – a good reason.

B 1 C'est un grand garçon aux cheveux roux et aux yeux bruns C'est un petit garçon aux cheveux noirs et aux yeux verts 3 C'est une grande fille aux cheveux bruns et aux yeux bruns 4 C'est une petite fille aux cheveux blonds et aux yeux bleus.

C **1** Elle porte une robe verte **2** Il porte une veste noire **3** Elle porte une jupe blanche **4** Il porte un blouson bleu.

E C'était . . . un bon restaurant   un bon hôtel   un long voyage   un livre intéressant   un mauvais film   une pièce intéressante.

Possessives

A mon bic; notre facture; vos collègues (tes collègues); mon (or ma) secrétaire; nos places; our colleagues; your bill; their seats; his (or her) colleagues; your ballpoint.

B **1f** Someone has stolen my driver's license **2d** We've lost our key **3b** I've lost my dentures **4c** This lady has broken her contact lenses **5a** Is this a photo of your daughter? **6e** Do we have to show our passports?

Demonstratives

A cette voiture-ci; ce restaurant-là; cet hôtel-ci; cette tasse-ci; cette voiture-là; ce bic-ci; ces comprimés-là; ces pneus-ci; ces chaussures-là; ces poires-ci.

B **1** Je préfère ces poires-là **2** J'aime ce restaurant-ci **3** J'ai besoin de ça **4** un bic comme ça.

Comparative and superlative

A plus ennuyeux; moins ennuyeux; plus commercialisé; moins affairé; le plus charmant; le plus difficile; le moins pratique; plus facile.

B Vous avez quelque chose de . . . plus fort? moins large? plus long? plus moderne? plus nouveau? moins pétillant? plus sombre? plus typique? moins clair?

C Nous prenons . . . le plus sec; le moins sec; le plus pétillant; le moins pétillant; le plus doux; le moins doux. Quel est le plus sec/le moins sec etc?

Adverbs

A C'est . . . très sucré; trop aigre; peu corsé; assez amer; trop sucré.

The word 'every'

A every Saturday; the whole season; the whole year; every two years; every thirty minutes; every quarter of an hour.

B **1** Il y a un métro tous les combien? – How often is there a subway? **2** La douleur revient toutes les dix minutes – The pain keeps coming back every ten minutes **3** Ma femme prend ce médicament toutes les six heures – My wife takes this medicine every six hours.

Prepositions

1 To/at/in

A **1** aéroport – Which is the bus that goes to the airport? **2** poubelles – I've got to go to the trash cans **3** plage – Do you stop at the beach? **4** Metz – Could you tell me the way to Metz, please? **5** parking – Are you going/Do you go to the parking lot?

B **1** Ma femme a mal *à* l'oreille – My wife's ear is aching **2** Mon fils a mal *aux* oreilles – My son's ears are aching **3** J'ai mal *aux* dents – I've got toothache **4** Mon mari a mal *à* la tête – My husband's got a headache **5** Ma fille a mal *au* dos – My daughter's got backache.

C **1** Regardez ma voiture! **2** Ecoutez mon mari! **3** Je cherche un parking **4** C'est moi qui paie la bière **5** en Espagne **6** à Strasbourg **7** au troisième étage **8** en autobus **9** un sandwich au jambon **10** le paquet à cinq francs **11** cinq timbres à deux francs.

2 Of/from

A **1c** dish of the day **2d** bargain of the year **3b** This gentleman comes from the U.S.A. **4e** I'll telephone you from Paris **5a** My wife comes from Portugal.

C **1e** near to Biarritz **2f** far from the center **3a** next to the harbor **4b** across the street from the toilets **5c** to the right of the church **6d** to the left of the supermarket.

D **1** C'est près du supermarché? **2** C'est loin de l'aéroport? **3** C'est près de Lille? **4** C'est en face du parking? **5** C'est à gauche des toilettes? **6** C'est devant la gare d'autobus?

Question words

A **1h** Do you accept American money? **2g** What's your house like? **3f** How long have you been on vacation? **4a** How many brothers do you have? **5b** To whom do I have to make the check payable? **6c** Can I pay with my Visa Card? **7d** The service is included, isn't it? **8e** How often is there a bus?

B **1** Vous vous appelez comment? **2** Vous habitez où? **3** Vous avez combien de sœurs? **4** Votre appartement est comment? **5** Il y a un métro tous les combien? **6** Vous acceptez les dollars? **7** Toutes les taxes sont comprises, n'est-ce pas? **8** Il faut faire le chèque à l'ordre de qui?

C **1** L'autobus pour Jarville part de quel arrêt? – Which stop does the bus for Jarville leave from? **2** Le train pour Thionville part de quel quai? – Which platform does the train for Thionville leave from? **3** Il faut prendre quelle ligne pour aller à Châtelet? – Which bus route (or subway line) do I have to take to get to Châtelet?

D (example only) **1** J'habite rue Washington, au numéro 37 (I live at 37 Washington Street) **2** Je suis né à Louisville **3** Je suis né le + date **4** J'ai . . . ans.

E Qu'est-ce que vous avez comme . . . hors d'œuvres; sandwiches; fromages; bières; vins; appartement; maison; voiture; journaux français?

Verb tables

These tables are designed for reference. Consult the section on verbs starting on p.15 for explanations.

Regular and irregular are convenient ways of classifying different types of verbs, but you will notice that irregular verbs have their own patterns too. This makes the job of learning them much easier.

In order to learn pronunciation you need access to a tape or French speaker, but the following guide may be useful:

a) these groups of final letters are not pronounced
   -e, -es, -ent, -s, -t

b) **-er, -ai, -ez** and **-é** are pronounced like the **A** in English *pay*

c) **-ais, -ait** and **-aient** are pronounced like the **E** in English *except*

REGULAR VERBS

-ER type   travailler (to work)

Present tense

je travaille	nous travaillons
tu travailles	vous travaillez
il travaille	ils travaillent

Future

je travaillerai	nous travaillerons
tu travailleras	vous travaillerez
il travaillera	ils travailleront

Imperfect

je travaillais	nous travaillions
tu travaillais	vous travailliez
il travaillait	ils travaillaient

Conditional

je travaillerais	nous travaillerions
tu travaillerais	vous travailleriez
il travaillerait	ils travailleraient

Perfect

j'ai travaillé	nous avons travaillé
tu as travaillé	vous avez travaillé
il a travaillé	ils ont travaillé

Commands

travaille!
travaillons!
travaillez!

Simple Past

il travailla	nous avons travaillé
	vous avez travaillé
ils travaillèrent	ils ont travaillé

-IR type   finir (to finish)

Present Tense

je finis	nous finissons
tu finis	vous finissez
il finit	ils finissent

Future

je finirai	nous finirons
tu finiras	vous finirez
il finira	ils finiront

Imperfect

je finissais	nous finissions
tu finissais	vous finissiez
il finissait	ils finissaient

Conditional

je finirais	nous finirions
tu finirais	vous finiriez
il finirait	ils finiraient

Perfect

j'ai fini	nous avons fini
tu as fini	vous avez fini
il a fini	ils ont fini

Commands

finis!
finissons!
finissez!

Simple Past

il finit	
ils finirent	

REGULAR VERBS – continued

-RE type   vendre (to sell)

Present Tense

je vends	nous vendons
tu vends	vous vendez
il vend	ils vendent

Future

je vendrai	nous vendrons
tu vendras	vous vendrez
il vendra	ils vendront

Imperfect

je vendais	nous vendions
tu vendais	vous vendiez
il vendait	ils vendaient

Conditional

je vendrais	nous vendrions
tu vendrais	vous vendriez
il vendrait	ils vendraient

Perfect

j'ai vendu	nous avons vendu
tu as vendu	vous avez vendu
il a vendu	ils ont vendu

Commands

vends!
vendons!
vendez!

Simple Past

il vendit	
ils vendirent	

REGULAR REFLEXIVE VERBS. Endings as above according to whether -er, -ir or -re type. An -er type is given in full as an example.

se dépêcher (to hurry)

Present

je me dépêche	nous nous dépêchons
tu te dépêches	vous vous dépêchez
il se dépêche	ils se dépêchent

Future

je me dépêcherai	nous nous dépêcherons
tu te dépêcheras	vous vous dépêcherez
il se dépêchera	ils se dépêcheront

Imperfect

je me dépêchais	nous nous dépêchions
tu te dépêchais	vous vous dépêchiez
il se dépêchait	ils se dépêchaient

Conditional

je me dépêcherais	nous nous dépêcherions
tu te dépêcherais	vous vous dépêcheriez
il se dépêcherait	ils se dépêcheraient

Perfect

je me suis dépêché	nous nous sommes dépêchés
tu t'es dépêché	vous vous êtes dépêchés
il s'est dépêché	ils se sont dépêchés

Commands

dépêche-toi!
dépêchons-nous!
dépêchez-vous!

Simple Past

il se dépêcha	
ils se dépêchèrent	

IRREGULAR VERBS. Where a tense is not given in full, assume the *endings* follow the same pattern as the ones given for regular *-er*, *-ir* and *-re* types. The column marked perfect reminds you whether the verb takes *avoir* or *être* in that tense and gives the past participle.

Infinitive	Present Tense	Imperfect	Perfect	Future	Conditional	Command	Simple Past
être (to be)	je suis tu es il est nous sommes vous êtes ils sont	j'étais tu étais il était nous étions vous étiez ils étaient	j'ai été tu as été etc.	je serai tu seras etc.	je serais tu serais etc.	sois! soyons! soyez!	il fut ils furent
avoir (to have)	j'ai tu as il a nous avons vous avez ils ont	j'avais tu avais il avait nous avions vous aviez ils avaient	j'ai eu tu as eu etc.	j'aurai tu auras etc.	j'aurais tu aurais etc.	aie! ayons! ayez!	il eut ils eurent
faire (to do, to make)	je fais tu fais il fait nous faisons vous faites ils font	je faisais tu faisais etc.	j'ai fait tu as fait etc.	je ferai tu feras etc.	je ferais tu ferais etc.	fais! faisons! faites!	il fit ils firent
aller (to go)	je vais tu vas il va nous allons vous allez ils vont	j'allais tu allais etc.	je suis allé tu es allé etc.	j'irai tu iras etc.	j'irais tu irais etc.	va! allons! allez!	il alla ils allèrent
devoir (to have to, to be obliged to, 'must')	je dois tu dois il doit nous devons vous devez ils doivent	je devais tu devais etc.	j'ai dû tu as dû etc.	je devrai tu devras etc.	je devrais tu devrais etc.	— — —	il dut ils durent
pouvoir (to be able, 'can')	je peux tu peux il peut nous pouvons vous pouvez ils peuvent	je pouvais tu pouvais etc.	j'ai pu tu as pu etc.	je pourrai tu pourras etc.	je pourrais tu pourrais etc.	— — —	il put ils purent
savoir (to know [how to])	je sais tu sais il sait nous savons vous savez ils savent	je savais tu savais etc.	j'ai su tu as su etc.	je saurai tu sauras etc.	je saurais tu saurais etc.	— — —	il sut ils surent
conduire (to drive)	je conduis tu conduis il conduit nous conduisons vous conduisez ils conduisent	je conduisais tu conduisais etc.	j'ai conduit tu as conduit etc.	je conduirai tu conduiras etc.	je conduirais tu conduirais etc.	conduis! conduisons! conduisez!	il conduisit ils conduisirent
connaître (to know, be familiar with)	je connais tu connais il connaît nous connaissons vous connaissez ils connaissent	je connaissais tu connaissais etc.	j'ai connu tu as connu etc.	je connaîtrai tu connaîtras etc.	je connaîtrais tu connaîtrais etc.	— — —	il connut ils connurent

IRREGULAR VERBS – continued

Infinitive	Present tense	Imperfect	Perfect	Future	Conditional	Command	Simple Past
reconnaître (to recognize)	exactly the same pattern as *connaître* but with *re-* as the first two letters — je reconnais, tu reconnais etc.						
disparaître (to disappear)	exactly the same pattern as *connaître* but with *dispar-* replacing *conn-* as the first letters — je disparais, tu disparais etc.						
ouvrir (to open)	j'ouvre, tu ouvres, il ouvre / nous ouvrons, vous ouvrez, ils ouvrent	j'ouvrais, tu ouvrais etc.	j'ai ouvert, tu as ouvert etc.	j'ouvrirai, tu ouvriras etc.	j'ouvrirais, tu ouvrirais etc.	ouvre! ouvrons! ouvrez!	il ouvrit, ils ouvrirent
mettre (to put)	je mets, tu mets, il met / nous mettons, vous mettez, ils mettent	je mettais, tu mettais etc.	j'ai mis, tu as mis etc.	je mettrai, tu mettras etc.	je mettrais, tu mettrais etc.	mets! mettons! mettez!	il mit, ils mirent
promettre (to promise)	exactly the same pattern as *mettre* with *pro-* as the first three letters						
prendre (to take)	je prends, tu prends, il prend / nous prenons, vous prenez, ils prennent	je prenais, tu prenais etc.	j'ai pris, tu as pris etc.	je prendrai, tu prendras etc.	je prendrais, tu prendrais etc.	prends! prenons! prenez!	il prit, ils prirent
comprendre (to understand)	exactly the same pattern as *prendre* with *com-* etc / je comprends, tu comprends etc						
apprendre (to learn)	exactly the same pattern as *prendre* with *ap-* as the first two letters / j'apprends, tu apprends etc.						
sortir (to go out)	je sors, tu sors, il sort / nous sortons, vous sortez, ils sortent	je sortais, tu sortais etc.	je suis sorti, tu es sorti etc.	je sortirai, tu sortiras etc.	je sortirais, tu sortirais etc.	sors! sortons! sortez!	il sortit, ils sortirent
partir (to depart)	je pars, tu pars, il part / nous partons, vous partez, ils partent	je partais, tu partais etc.	je suis parti, tu es parti etc.	je partirai, tu partiras etc.	je partirais, tu partirais etc.	pars! partons! partez!	il partit, ils partirent
dormir (to sleep)	je dors, tu dors, il dort / nous dormons, vous dormez, ils dorment	je dormais, tu dormais etc.	j'ai dormi, tu as dormi etc.	je dormirai, tu dormiras etc.	je dormirais, tu dormirais etc.	dors! dormons! dormez!	il dormit, ils dormirent

IRREGULAR VERBS – continued

Infinitive	Present tense	Imperfect	Perfect	Future	Conditional	Command	Simple Past
servir (to serve)	je sers tu sers il sert nous servons vous servez ils servent	je servais tu servais etc.	j'ai servi tu as servi etc.	je servirai tu serviras etc.	je servirais tu servirais etc.	sers! servons! servez!	il servit ils servirent
recevoir (to receive)	je reçois tu reçois il reçoit nous recevons vous recevez ils reçoivent	je recevais tu recevais etc.	j'ai reçu tu as reçu etc.	je recevrai tu recevras etc.	je recevrais tu recevrais etc.	reçois! recevons! recevez!	il reçut ils reçurent
vouloir (to want, wish)	je veux tu veux il veut nous voulons vous voulez ils veulent	je voulais tu voulais etc.	j'ai voulu tu as voulu etc.	je voudrai tu voudras etc.	je voudrais tu voudrais etc.	— — —	il voulut ils voulurent
venir (to come)	je viens tu viens il vient	nous venons vous venez ils viennent	je venais tu venais etc.	je suis venu tu es venu etc.	je viendrai tu viendras etc.	je viendrais tu viendrais etc.	viens! venons! venez!	il vint ils vinrent
boire (to drink)	je bois tu bois il boit nous buvons vous buvez ils boivent	je buvais tu buvais etc.	j'ai bu tu as bu etc.	je boirai tu boiras etc.	je boirais tu boirais etc.	bois! buvons! buvez!	il but ils burent
voir (to see)	je vois tu vois il voit nous voyons vous voyez ils voient	je voyais tu voyais etc.	j'ai vu tu as vu etc.	je verrai tu verras etc.	je verrais tu verrais etc.	vois! voyons! voyez!	il vit ils virent
écrire (to write)	j'écris tu écris il écrit nous écrivons vous écrivez ils écrivent	j'écrivais tu écrivais etc.	j'ai écrit tu as écrit etc.	j'écrirai tu écriras etc.	j'écrirais tu écrirais etc.	écris! écrivons! écrivez!	il écrit ils écrivirent
dire (to say to tell)	je dis tu dis il dit nous disons vous dites ils disent	je disais tu disais etc.	j'ai dit tu as dit etc.	je dirai tu diras etc.	je dirais tu dirais etc.	dis! disons! dites!	il dit ils dirent
falloir (to be necessary)	il faut	il fallait	il a fallu	il faudra	il faudrait	—	il fallut
pleuvoir (to rain)	il pleut	il pleuvait	il a plu	il pleuvra	il pleuvrait	—	il plut

Grammar Index

Topic Index